MICROWAVE MEALS
IN MINUTES

D1339949

MICROWAVE MEALS IN MINUTES

Quick to Prepare – Easy to Cook

Mary Norwak

Edited by Daphne Metland

W. Foulsham & Co. Ltd.

London · New York · Toronto · Cape Town · Sydney

W. FOULSHAM & COMPANY LIMITED
Yeovil Road, Slough, Berkshire, SL1 4JH

ISBN 0-572-01343-4

Printed in Great Britain
at St. Edmundsbury Press,
Bury St. Edmunds.

CONTENTS

INTRODUCTION

Fast food has become synonymous with junk food, but it does not have to be. A microwave oven can be a great time saver in the kitchen for busy families, or for people who need to prepare a meal after a hard day's work.

As well as defrosting quick snacks and baking the occasional potato in its jacket, a microwave can be used for 'real' cooking and it is here that the greatest time savings can be made; Sunday lunch in under an hour, a weekday meal in 30 minutes and a cooked breakfast within 15 minutes.

Allow a little while to become used to slightly different cooking methods needed with a microwave oven. Most of us learned to cook at our mother's knee and gradually absorbed the information needed over the years; with a microwave oven many techniques need revising and although at first this seems time consuming, after a while it becomes second nature again.

It is worth placing the microwave near the main worktop area, so that you can keep half an eye on the food at first and learn to trust your own judgement, just as you would with a conventional cooker. A collection of suitable dishes in glass, china or plastic are useful and soon you find which are most often used. Work with the dishes you already have to begin with and then see which new ones would be useful.

Don't forget the microwave is a very good timesaver for all sorts of odd jobs in the kitchen, like softening butter for cake making, melting chocolate, or jellies, even warming flour for bread making.

There are some jobs the microwave oven will not do as well as an ordinary cooker, such as frying, baking and cooking pastry. Other dishes look different but taste the same. This may or may not matter to you and your family. There are lots of simple ways to improve the appearance of foods, which are included in this book. Use the microwave along with your conventional cooker to get the best of both worlds and save your time and energy in the kitchen.

USING A MICROWAVE OVEN

The energy in a microwave oven is a type of high frequency radio wave. Microwaves are safe and do not damage cells, or alter the structure of food. Food is composed of water molecules and as microwaves enter the food they cause these molecules to vibrate at over 2000 million times a second, and the friction generates heat in the food. Microwaves penetrate from all sides to a depth of 1½–2 ins/3.8–5 cm, generating heat on the outside layers of the food which spreads by conduction to the centre. **This accounts for the 'standing time' often given in recipes, as food continues to cook for a few minutes after it has been taken from the oven. It is therefore very important not to overcook food such as cakes, which look undercooked when taken from the oven but which firm up after a few minutes' standing time**. Since there is no applied surface heat, however, food does not brown during short cooking times, although it will take place when a long cooking time is involved, such as in preparing poultry or a joint of meat. To counteract this, microwave recipes often suggest applying a rich baste, or sprinkling with spice or herbs, or spreading with icing, to disguise the paleness of food. Microwave browning spices are now available for savoury foods. A browning element, like a grill, is fitted into some expensive microwave cookers and may be used to pre-brown food or to brown it after or during cooking. A browning dish is useful too.

You will find that many of your cooked dishes, particularly cakes and breads, look a little different from those cooked in conventional ovens. Do not be tempted to add extra cooking time, as this will make the food hard and unpalatable.

To provide 'eye appeal' cakes may be iced, sweet dishes may be sprinkled with sugar or chocolate, and savoury dishes with herbs and spices.

Power control

The most basic models operate on constant full or high power. Variable control ovens enable power to be reduced to low or medium, which may be expressed in numbers, or labelled as 'simmer', 'reheat', 'roast', etc. A 'defrost' control button enables food to be thawed by exposing it to microwave energy for a short period, then allowing a 'standing' time, and repeating the processes as required without manual control. Consult your manufacturer's booklet to see what is the recommended cooking procedure for each labelled control. The 'defrost' control for instance may also be used for finishing slow-cooking stews; the 'simmering' control is also suitable for cooking delicate dishes such as eggs.

Preparation of food

Food will be heated or cooked faster if it is at room temperature. Chilled food will take longer to cook. Frozen foods may be defrosted first and then cooked, while some frozen foods such as vegetables may be cooked straight from the freezer. Most of the recipes in this book can be frozen, and the recommended freezing time is given after the freezing symbol (✳). I have also included any special instructions to take into account before freezing the dish, together with thawing or reheating times.

Very dense food will take longer to cook than lighter dishes. If a ring mould is used for cooking a cake or pudding, this will help to transmit the microwaves to the centre. A dense piece of meat will take longer than minced or chopped meat. Food should be formed into the neatest shape possible so that microwaves are absorbed evenly, and for this reason a rolled joint of meat is preferable to an irregularly shaped joint. Poultry should have legs and wings tucked in closely to the body. Food which is in a thin single layer will heat better than food which is piled up. Protect thin pieces like chicken drumsticks with small pieces of foil, and tuck fish tails under to make a double thickness.

Foods with a skin such as apples, potatoes and egg yolks, should be pierced before cooking to prevent exploding. If clingfilm is used to cover food, it should be pierced in two places to allow steam to escape.

Some recipes recommend that food should be stirred, and this is necessary to distribute heat in the food. For the same reason, pieces of food may have to be rearranged in their container during cooking. You simply switch off, take the food out and stir or rearrange it.

Timing

Cooking times in the microwave oven vary very slightly, just as they do in an ordinary oven. However because microwave cooking times are so short, results can be altered by cooking for an extra 30–60 seconds.

The cooking times quoted are a guide and it is important to undercook food and allow it to stand where necessary. The shape and density of the food, the dish it is cooked in and the quantity of food being cooked will all affect the results. Even something as simple as cooking frozen peas will be affected by the sort of dish they are cooked in. Choose a flat shallow pie dish and they will cook more quickly than if placed in a small deep dish.

Use the times quoted as a guide, but also cook by eye. This in fact is how we cook in a conventional cooker. We open the oven door and look and leave the food for an extra five minutes or so, if necessary. Do just the same with your microwave, but remember to think in terms of seconds instead of minutes. Overcooking results in dry unpalatable food. Undercook, and the food can be returned to the microwave for an extra minute or two after standing, if necessary.

TIME ADJUSTMENT

The recipes in this book have been tested with a 600 watt output microwave oven and times are given accordingly.

For a 500 watt oven increase timing by about 25 seconds for each minute.

For a 700 watt oven decrease by about 25 seconds for each minute.

For a variable control oven adjust to a suitable power level.

COOKING EQUIPMENT

A very wide range of materials may be used in the microwave oven. One of the advantages is that food may often be cooked in its serving dish, which eliminates a great deal of washing-up. Although so many pieces of equipment may be used, however, it is very important to avoid metal, and also to choose the correctly shaped dish.

Metal

Metal dishes, trimmings or parts of dishes can cause arcing in the microwave oven which creates flashes of light and reflects the microwaves so that they will not penetrate the food. No metal dishes, baking trays, cast-iron casseroles or foil dishes should be used. Be particularly careful that there are no metal screws or handles on non-metal containers. A metallic decoration on a plate or mug can also cause the same problem, and so can metal twist-ties on freezer packs and cook-bags. Check with the manufacturer's instruction book though, as some allow small quantities of foil to be used.

Other materials

Ovenproof and ordinary glass, pottery and china may all be used. This means that a meal may be heated on a dinner plate, for instance. Pottery casseroles and baking dishes may be used. Plastic dishes which are suitable for a dishwasher are also suitable for the microwave oven, but food with a high fat or sugar content becomes very hot and may melt plastic dishes. Paper towels, cartons and pulp board are suitable for cooking and will absorb excess fat from the food, but wax-coated paper should not be used as the coating may melt. Freezer boil-in-bags and roasting bags are excellent for microwave cooking as they prevent food spattering and making a mess in the oven, but they should be closed with a twist of string or an elastic band

and not with a metal-based twist-tie. Allow plenty of space in the bag a some foods give off steam. Small bags will need to be punctured to release the air. Do not use melamine containers in the oven, as they absorb the heat and may char. Soft polythene containers may melt, as will yoghurt or cottage cheese containers.

Is the container suitable?

As a test to see if a container is suitable for the microwave oven, stand a glass of cold water in or next to the container being tested. Microwave for 1½ minutes. If the container feels cool and the water hot, then it is suitable for microwave use. If the container and water feel warm, the container is only suitable for short term heating as it is absorbing energy. If the container is warm and the water cool, then it is not suitable for microwave use.

Shapes

A round container gives the best results as an oval one will allow the food to cook more quickly at the narrow ends. Large shallow dishes are better than tall deep ones so that the heat spreads evenly through the food. Liquids, however, are better heated in a tall narrow container such as a jug, which should be large enough to allow for liquid boiling and rising. A straight-sided container is better than a curved one so that the microwaves penetrate more evenly, but the food must be stirred several times or it will overcook in the corners.

Special Microwave Containers

Ranges of rigid permanent microwave ware, freezer to microwave ware and ovenboard microwave dishes are available. Many users find some of these useful, but it should not be necessary to buy a complete new range when you buy a microwave oven. Start with your existing glass and china dishes and add extra ones as necessary.

Browning Dish

This is a ceramic dish, coated with a tin-oxide layer that absorbs the microwave energy and heats up. It should be preheated, empty, in the microwave, usually for about 8 minutes. Food then placed on the hot surface will sear and brown. Ideal for steaks, chops and sausages etc., and a useful addition, as it extends the range of foods that can be prepared in the microwave. It can also be used as an ordinary dish in the microwave without preheating.

The preheating time sounds a disadvantage, but make it a habit to put the dish in the oven to preheat while you prepare the ingredients and it will not waste time.

Timings Conversion Table

Please note that all the timings in this book are based on a 600 watt microwave oven. If you have a 500 watt or 700 watt oven you can convert the timings easily using this chart. All timings are approximate – and remember, it is better to undercook than overcook as dishes can always be returned to the microwave for a few more seconds.

500 watt	600 watt	700 watt
45s	30s	15s
1m 25s	1m	35s
2m 50s	2m	1m 15s
4m 15s	3m	1m 45s
5m 40s	4m	2m 20s
7m	5m	3m
8m 30s	6m	3m 30s
10m	7m	4m
11m 20s	8m	4m 40s
12m 45s	9m	5m 15s
14m	10m	6m
15m 35s	11m	6m 40s
17m	12m	7m
18m 25s	13m	7m 35s
19m 50s	14m	8m
21m 15s	15m	8m 45s
22m 40s	16m	9m 15s
24m	17m	9m 50s
25m 30s	18m	10m 30s
27m	19m	11m
28m 20s	20m	11m 40s
29m 45s	21m	12m 15s
32m 35s	22m	12m 45s
34m	23m	13m 20s
35m 25s	24m	14m
35m 50s	25m	14m 35s
37m 15s	26m	15m
38m 40s	27m	15m 35s
40m	28m	16m 15s
41m 25s	29m	16m 45s
42m 50s	30m	17m 20s

COOKING FRESH FOOD

VEGETABLES

Vegetables may be cooked in a glass casserole dish or microwave dish, or in a roasting bag. They need to be

Vegetable	Quantity or weight
Artichoke (globe)	*1 medium*
Artichoke (Jerusalem)	*1 lb./450 g.*
Asparagus	*1 lb./450 g. medium spears*
Broad beans	*1 lb./450 g. shelled*
Broccoli	*1 lb./450 g. sprigs*
Brussels sprouts	*8 oz./225 g.*
Cabbage	*1 lb./450 g. shredded*
Carrots	*8 oz./225 g. new whole or old sliced*
Cauliflower	*8 oz./225 g. florets*
Celery	*12 oz./350 g. sliced*
Corn-on-the-cob	*2 medium, husked*
	1 cob
	2 cobs
Courgettes	*1 lb./whole sliced*
French beans	*1 lb./450 g. whole*
Leeks	*1 lb./450 g. sliced*
Mushrooms	*8 oz./225 g. unpeeled*
Onions	*1 lb./450 g. quartered*
Parsnips	*1 lb./450 g. diced*
Peas	*1 lb./450 g. shelled*
Potatoes	*1 lb./450 g. new scraped*
	1 lb./450 g. old cut in pieces
(for baking)	*2 lb./900 g. scrubbed*

prepared as for conventional cooking, and then have the addition of a little water or butter.

Treatment	Cooking time
Remove stem and trim leaves. Add 4 tablespoons water	*9 minutes*
Peel finely. Add 1 oz./25 g. butter and 2 tablespoons water	*11 minutes*
Add 2 tablespoons water	*8 minutes*
Add 2 tablespoons water	*7 minutes*
Add 4 tablespoons water	*9 minutes*
Add 2 tablespoons water	*8 minutes*
Add 2 tablespoons water	*10 minutes*
Add 2 tablespoons water	*10 minutes*
Add 4 tablespoons water	*5 minutes*
Add 2 tablespoons water	*9 minutes*
Add 1/2 oz./15 g. butter and 2 tablespoons water	*10 minutes*
—	*8 minutes*
—	*11 minutes*
Add 1 oz./25 g. butter	*4 minutes*
Add 3 tablespoons water	*8 minutes*
Add 1 oz./25 g. butter	*8 minutes*
Add 1 oz./25 g. butter	*2 minutes*
—	*8 minutes*
Add 2 tablespoons water	*10 minutes*
Add 2 tablespoons water	*8 minutes*
Add 4 tablespoons water	*5 minutes*
Add 3 tablespoons water	*6 minutes*
Place on kitchen paper	*20 minutes*

Vegetable	Quantity or weight
Peppers	*8 oz./225 g. diced*
Runner beans	*1 lb./450 g. sliced*
Ratatouille	*1 lb./450 g.*
	8 oz./225 g.
Spinach	*1 lb./450 g.*
Spring greens	*1 lb./450 g.*
Swedes and turnips	*1 lb./450 g. diced*

MEAT

Joints can be difficult to cook in the microwave oven because they are irregular in shape. A leg of lamb for instance is much thicker at one end, so the thinner end will overcook. It is therefore best, if possible, to bone and roll a joint and tie it into a uniform shape. Like poultry, meat may be cooked for preference in a large roasting bag which will prevent spattering and will help the meat to achieve brownness.

Meat	Cooking time
Pork, lamb, ham, veal	*9 minutes per 1 lb./450 g.*
Beef: rare	*6 minutes per 1 lb./450 g.*
medium	*7 minutes per 1 lb./450 g.*
well-done	*8 minutes per 1 lb./450 g.*

POULTRY

Whole birds and portions may be cooked quickly in the microwave oven, but a little care is needed in preparation. Be sure that birds or portions are completely defrosted, then rinsed in cold water and dried well. Poultry should not be cooked uncovered or it will dry out, and also splash grease in the oven. To achieve a brown skin, baste the bird before cooking with 1 oz./25 g./2 tablespoons melted butter into which 1 teaspoon soy sauce, 1 teaspoon Worcestershire sauce, and 1 teaspoon paprika have been stirred. Place in a large roasting bag and tie with string or an elastic band, leaving plenty of room

Treatment	Cooking time
Add ½ oz./15 g. butter	2 minutes
Add 3 tablespoons water	6 minutes
Add 1 oz./25 g. butter	9 minutes
Add ½ oz./15 g. butter	5 minutes
—	7 minutes
—	8 minutes
Add 2 tablespoons water	10 minutes

round the bird in the bag. Stand the bag on a large plate. Cook for the given time and then drain off juices to use for gravy. Wrap the bird in foil and leave to stand for 20 minutes before carving.

N.B. Cooking time for game (rabbit or hare) is as for chicken.

Bird	Cooking time
Chicken and turkey	8 minutes per 1 lb./450 g.
Duck	9 minutes per 1 lb./450 g.

FISH

Fresh fish may be cooked quickly in the microwave oven. No liquid is needed, but a small knob of butter may be placed on each piece of fish. A little lemon juice may be added to white fish. Season after cooking.

Fish	Quantity or weight	Cooking time
White fish (cod, haddock, plaice)	1 lb./450 g. prepared fillets, cutlets or steaks	8 minutes
Oily fish (mackerel, trout, herring)	1 lb./450 g. whole and gutted fish	6 minutes
Smoked fish (cod, haddock)	1 lb./450 g. prepared fillets, cutlets or steaks	7 minutes
Kipper fillets	1 lb./450 g.	4 minutes

FRUIT

Fruit cooks well in the microwave oven and is full of flavour. Liquid is not needed for most fruit, but white or brown sugar may be sprinkled on before cooking.

Fruit	Quantity or weight
Apples	*1 lb./450 g.*
Apricots	*1 lb./450 g.*
Gooseberries	*1 lb./450 g.*
Peaches	*4 medium*
Pears	*6 medium*
Plums and greengages	*1 lb./450 g.*
Rhubarb	*1 lb./450 g.*

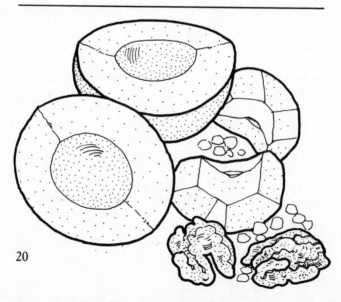

Flavourings such as liqueurs or spices may be stirred in when the fruit has cooked. Cook fruit in a container covered with clingfilm with two small slits cut in the film.

Treatment	Cooking time
Peel, core and cut in slices. Sprinkle with sugar	*7 minutes*
Cut in half and remove stones. Sprinkle with sugar	*8 minutes*
Top and tail. Sprinkle with sugar	*4 minutes*
Cut in half and remove stones. Sprinkle with sugar	*4 minutes*
Peel, halve and core. Add 3 oz./75 g. sugar dissolved in 6 tablespoons hot water	*8 minutes*
Cut in half and remove stones. Sprinkle with sugar	*4 minutes*
Cut in 1 in./2.5 cm. lengths Sprinkle with sugur	*10 minutes*

COOKING FROZEN VEGETABLES

Always cook frozen vegetables without thawing so that they keep their colour, flavour and texture. Put salt or other seasonings at the bottom of the dish as it may dehydrate them if sprinkled on top (the seasoning will be distributed when vegetables are stirred). Put free-flowing vegetables in a shallow dish so that they form an even layer; large irregular vegetables such as broccoli should be arranged with the thickest parts facing outwards to the edge of the dish. If vegetables are in a block, separate half-way through cooking.

Very little liquid is needed to cook frozen vegetables, so do not increase the amount of water given below. Stir vegetables once or twice during cooking so that they cook evenly; they will also cook more evenly if covered with clingfilm which should have two small slits cut in it to release steam. When vegetables are cooked, they may be tossed with butter or cream and herbs, and if covered will keep warm for 10 minutes, so that another vegetable may be cooked during this time, or some sauce or gravy made.

Vegetable	Treatment	Cooking time
Broad beans, sliced beans,	3 tablespoons water	9 minutes (1 lb./450 g.)
Broccoli spears, Brussels sprouts, carrots, courgettes, peas, sweetcorn kernels	1 tablespoon water	5 minutes (8 oz./225 g.)
Asparagus, cauliflower sprigs	3 tablespoons water	10 minutes (1 lb./450 g.)
Whole or thick-cut beans	1 tablespoon water	6 minutes (8 oz./225 g.)

COOKING CONVENIENCE FOODS

Convenience foods are truly convenient when a microwave oven can be used for defrosting and/or cooking rapidly. Home-frozen raw materials and complete dishes, and their commercial equivalents, can be quickly placed on the table and this considerably widens the choice of food for menus when cooking time is limited in a busy family. If foods are packed in foil, it is important to transfer to a microwave dish or non-metal serving dish; food packed in a polythene bag may, however, be defrosted and/or cooked in this container.

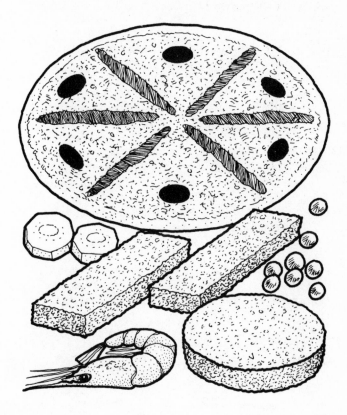

DEFROSTING

If your microwave oven has a 'defrost' setting, consult the manufacturer's instruction booklet for timing. If this is not available, use the 'cooking' setting, following this chart. Raw materials which have been defrosted (e.g. meat) may then be cooked by conventional methods such as grilling or roasting, or cooking may continue in the microwave oven. Some raw materials such as vegetables and fish need not be defrosted, but may be cooked from the frozen state in the microwave oven, and this of course applies to ready-frozen complete dishes. Instructions for these will be found on page 30 in the cooking chart.

Instructions for poultry (whole) and joints of meat will be found on page 27.

Food	Quantity or weight	Defrosting time
Bread	Large loaf	Defrost 2 minutes. Let stand 6 minutes. Defrost 2 minutes
	Single slice	Defrost ¾–1¼ minutes depending on thickness
Pastry (puff)	14 oz./400 g.	Leave in wrapping. Defrost 2 minutes
	8 oz./225 g.	Defrost 1 minute
Pastry (shortcrust)	14 oz./400 g.	Defrost 2 minutes
	8 oz./225 g.	Defrost 1 minute
Fish steaks	3½ oz./90 g.	Cover with clingfilm. Defrost 3½ minutes. Let stand 5 minutes
Fish fingers	10	Remove from pack. Defrost 4 minutes. Let stand 2 minutes
Fish cakes	2	Remove from pack. Defrost 2½ minutes. Let stand 3 minutes

Food	Quantity or weight	Defrosting time
White fish (e.g. cod, haddock, plaice)	*1 lb./450 g. prepared cutlets, fillets or steaks*	*Cover with clingfilm. Defrost 5 minutes*
Oily fish (e.g. herring, mackerel, trout)	*1 lb./450 g. whole gutted fish*	*Cover with clingfilm. Defrost 3 minutes*
Smoked fish (e.g. haddock, cod, kipper)	*1 lb./450 g. fillets*	*Cover with clingfilm. Defrost 3 minutes*
	1 lb./450 g. cutlets or steaks	*Cover with clingfilm. Defrost 4 minutes*
Chops (lamb and pork)	*2 medium (5 oz./125 g. each)*	*Defrost 2 minutes. Let stand 2 minutes*
Liver	*8 oz./225 g.*	*Heat 2 minutes. Let stand 5 minutes*
Minced beef	*8 oz./225 g.*	*Defrost 1½ minutes. Let stand 5 minutes. Defrost 1½ minutes. Let stand 5 minutes*
Chicken joints	*8 oz./225 g.*	*Defrost 3 minutes. Let stand 5 minutes*
Game pieces	*8oz./225 g.*	*Defrost 3 minutes. Let stand 5 minutes*
Sausages	*4 large*	*Defrost 1 minute. Separate. Defrost 1 minute. Let stand 2 minutes*
Roast beef in gravy	*4 oz./100 g.*	*Remove from foil pack. Defrost 2 minutes. Let stand 2 minutes*

Food	Quantity or weight	Defrosting time
Roast beef in gravy	*12 oz./350 g.*	*Remove from foil pack. Defrost 3 minutes. Let stand 3 minutes*
Whipped cream	*1/2 pint/300 ml./ 1 1/4 cups*	*Remove lid. Defrost 1 minute. Let stand 10 minutes*
Cheesecake	*Family size*	*Remove from foil pack. Defrost 1 1/2 minutes. Let stand 15 minutes*
Mousse tub	*Individual size*	*Remove lid. Defrost 20 seconds*
Trifle tub	*Individual size*	*Remove lid. Defrost 35 seconds*
Dairy cream sponge	*1*	*Remove carton. Defrost 40 seconds. Let stand 5 minutes*
Cream doughnuts	*3*	*Remove carton. Defrost 35 seconds*
Jam doughnuts	*2*	*Remove carton. Defrost 1 1/2 minutes*
Cream eclairs	*4*	*Remove carton. Defrost 45 seconds. Let stand 10 minutes*

POULTRY (WHOLE) AND
JOINTS OF MEAT

Whole birds and joints of meat should be thawed on the 'defrost' setting, and time must be allowed for 'standing' so that heat penetrates the food without cooking it.

For chicken joints, chops and minced beef, see page 25.

Food	Quantity or weight	Defrosting time
Chicken	*2–3 lb./900 g.– 1.5 kg.*	*Defrost 10 minutes. Let stand 20 minutes. Defrost 5 minutes. Let stand 10 minutes*
Game (whole)	*2–3 lb. 900 g.–1.5 kg.*	*Defrost 10 minutes Let stand 20 minutes. Defrost 5 minutes. Let stand 10 minutes*
Duck	*4½ lb./2 kg.*	*Defrost 10 minutes. Let stand 30 minutes. Defrost 6 minutes. Let stand 15 minutes*
Turkey	*13 lb./6 kg.*	*Defrost 20 minutes. Let stand 30 minutes. Defrost 10 minutes. Let stand 20 minutes*
Beef: joints on bone	*3 lb./1.5 kg.*	*Defrost 10 minutes. Let stand 20 minutes. Defrost 5 minutes. Let stand 20 minutes*
rolled joints	*3 lb./1.5 kg.*	*Defrost 10 minutes. Let stand 20 minutes. Defrost 5 minutes. Let stand 10 minutes*

Food		Quantity or weight	Defrosting time
	stewing meat	2 lb./900 g.	Defrost 5 minutes. Let stand 10 minutes. Defrost 2½ minutes. Let stand 5 minutes
	grilling meat	2 lb./900 g.	Defrost 4 minutes. Let stand 5 minutes. Defrost 4 minutes. Let stand 10 minutes
Veal:	roasting joints	3 lb./1.5 kg.	Defrost 5 minutes. Let stand 10 minutes. Defrost 5 minutes. Let stand 10 minutes
Lamb:	joints on bone	5 lb./2.2 kg.	Defrost 10 minutes. Let stand 20 minutes. Defrost 5 minutes. Let stand 10 minutes.
	chops	2 medium (5 oz./125 g. each)	Defrost 2½ minutes. Let stand 5 minutes. Defrost 2½ minutes
		4 medium (5 oz./125 g. each)	Defrost 5 minutes. Let stand 10 minutes. Defrost 2½ minutes. Let stand 5 minutes
Pork:	leg roast	5 lb./2.2 kg.	Defrost 10 minutes. Let stand 30 minutes. Defrost 5 minutes. Let stand 20 minutes
	loin roast	3 lb./1.5 kg.	Defrost 10 minutes. Let stand 20 minutes. Defrost 5 minutes. Let stand 10 minutes

Food	Quantity or weight	Defrosting time
chops	*2 medium (5 oz./125 g. each)*	*Defrost 2½ minutes. Let stand 5 minutes. Defrost 2½ minutes*
	4 medium (5 oz./125 g. each)	*Defrost 5 minutes. Let stand 10 minutes. Defrost 2½ minutes. Let stand 5 minutes*
sausagemeat	*1 lb./450 g.*	*Defrost 2½ minutes. Let stand 10 minutes. Defrost 2½ minutes*

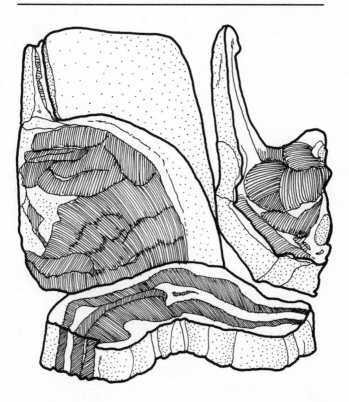

REHEATING FROZEN FOOD

If you have prepared cooked dishes for the freezer yourself, it is of course easy to see that they are packed in non-metallic dishes. Dishes are available in which food may be cooked in a microwave, frozen and then later reheated. Food may also of course be cooked in a conventional oven in everyday dishes or tins, and can then be transferred to microwave packaging for freezing and reheating. If a commercially prepared dish is packed in foil, the food must be transferred to a non-metal container before defrosting and/or reheating. It is important that the food should just fit into the new dish, as, if the dish is too wide, the outside of the food will defrost and cover the base of the container, and will then start cooking while the main block of food is still being defrosted. Food which is packed in a boil-in-bag pouch may, however, be cooked in this packaging.

Food	Quantity or weight
Fish in sauce	*6 oz./150 g. portion*
Fish cakes	*4 × 2 oz./50 g. each*
Meat casserole	*4 portions*
Shepherd's pie	*4 portions*
Meat pies (cooked filling, uncooked pastry)	*4 × 2 oz./50 g. each*
Spaghetti sauce	*4 portions*
Soup	*2 pints/1.2 l.*

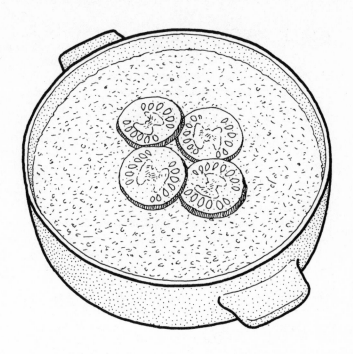

Treatment	Cooking time
Pierce bag	*5 minutes*
Shallow dish	*4 minutes. Turn over once*
Casserole dish	*10 minutes. Break up block twice during heating*
Casserole dish	*10 minutes. Cover with foil and let stand 5 minutes*
Square dish	*6 minutes. Turn pies around two or three times*
Casserole dish	*12 minutes. Break up block as it heats*
Boil-in-bag placed in bowl	*18 minutes*

QUICKTIPS

1. *Cocktail snacks*   Make potato crisps and cocktail biscuits crisp again by heating 15 seconds in microwave. Let stand 15 seconds.

2. *Citrus fruit*   Warm 10 seconds in microwave so that fruit is easy to squeeze and yields more juice.

3. *Coffee*   Refrigerate left over coffee (made with coffee beans). For a fresh-tasting cup of coffee, pour into cup or mug and heat 1–1½ minutes in microwave.

4. *Leftover pies*   Refrigerate leftover cold fruit pies. Put individual portion on plate and heat 1 minute in microwave.

5. *Biscuits*   If they have softened, arrange a few in single layer on plate and microwave for 30 seconds.

6. *Dried herbs*   Place a few sprigs of herbs or leaves between two pieces of kitchen paper. Microwave 2 minutes until dry and crumbly. Store in jars.

7. *Flaming puddings*   To ignite Christmas pudding, etc., put brandy into a glass measure and heat 15 seconds in microwave. Pour over pudding and ignite.

8. *Blanched nuts*   Heat ½ pint/300 ml./1¼ cups water in measuring jug for about 2 minutes until boiling. Add nuts and heat 45 seconds. Drain well, and slip off skins by rubbing with kitchen paper.

9. *Toasted nuts*   Put blanched nuts in shallow dish with butter and heat 2–3 minutes until nuts are lightly browned, stirring occasionally.

10. *Softening dried fruit*   Put hard dried fruit in shallow dish. Sprinkle with 1 teaspoon water. Cover and heat 20 seconds.

11. *Juice concentrate*   Remove frozen concentrated juice from can and put in jug. Heat 30 seconds until soft and mix with water.

SOUPS AND STARTERS

Borsch

✳ 2 months   Serves 4

INGREDIENTS	Imperial	Metric	American
Beetroot (raw)	12 oz.	350 g.	12 oz.
Water	1 pt.	600 ml.	2½ cups
Salt and freshly ground black pepper			
Sugar	½ oz.	15 g.	1 tbsp.
Lemon juice	2 tbsp.	2 tbsp.	2 tbsp.
Soured cream	¼ pt.	150 ml.	⅔ cup

Wash and scrape the beetroot. Grate them coarsely. Put into a non-metal casserole with water, salt, pepper, sugar and lemon juice. Cover with lid and microwave for 12 minutes. Remove from microwave, cool and then chill completely. Serve cold with a spoonful of soured cream in each bowl.

SPECIAL INSTRUCTIONS
Freeze without sour cream.

THAW
At room temperature 3 hours

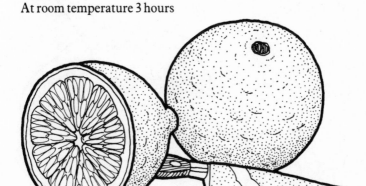

Green Pea Soup

✳ 2 months   Serves 4

INGREDIENTS	Imperial	Metric	American
Butter	*1 oz.*	*25 g.*	*2 tbsp.*
Onion	*1 medium*	*1 medium*	*1 medium*
Frozen peas	*12 oz.*	*350 g.*	*12 oz.*
Salt and freshly ground black pepper			
Sugar	*1 tsp.*	*1 tsp.*	*1 tsp.*
Chicken stock	*1 pt.*	*600 ml.*	*2¼ cups*
Single cream	*¼ pt.*	*150 ml.*	*⅔ cup*
Chopped mint	*1 tbsp.*	*1 tbsp.*	*1 tbsp.*

Put the butter and finely chopped onion into a bowl and heat in the microwave oven for 3 minutes, stirring once. Add the peas, salt, pepper, sugar and hot stock. Heat in microwave 5 minutes. Put through a sieve or blend in a liquidiser. Reheat in microwave oven for 2 minutes. Stir in the cream and serve at once, with a little mint sprinkled on each portion.

SPECIAL INSTRUCTIONS
Freeze without cream and mint. Add just before serving.

REHEAT
18 minutes

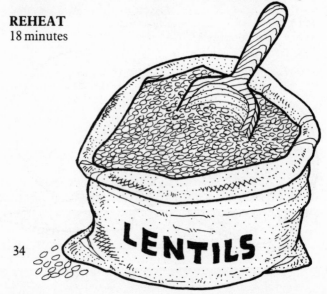

Tomato Soup

* 2 months Serves 4

INGREDIENTS	Imperial	Metric	American
Onion	1	1	1
Celery stick	1	1	1
Tomatoes	1 lb.	450 g.	1 lb.
Butter	1 oz.	25 g.	2 tbsp.
Plain flour	1 oz.	25 g.	2 tbsp.
Chicken stock	1 pt.	600 ml.	2½ cups
Tomato purée	2 tbsp.	2 tbsp.	2 tbsp.
Salt and freshly ground black pepper			
Basil	1 tsp.	1 tsp.	1 tsp.
Whipped cream	¼ pt.	150 ml.	⅔ cup
Chopped parsley	1 tbsp.	1 tbsp.	1 tbsp.

Chop the onion and celery finely. Skin the tomatoes, remove seeds, and chop the flesh. Put the butter into a bowl and heat in the microwave for 30 seconds. Add onion and celery and continue cooking for 5 minutes. Add the tomatoes and cook for 2 minutes. Stir in the flour and hot chicken stock with the tomato purée. Cook in the microwave oven for 5 minutes and then season well. Serve in bowls with a spoonful of cream and a sprinkling of parsley on each portion.

SPECIAL INSTRUCTIONS
Freeze without cream and parsley. Add just before serving.

REHEAT
18 minutes

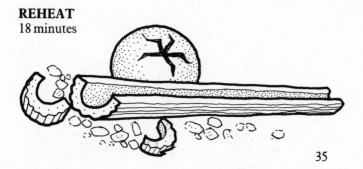

Chicken Liver Pâté

✳ 2 months   Serves 4

INGREDIENTS	Imperial	Metric	American
Onion	*1 medium*	*1 medium*	*1 medium*
Garlic clove	*1*	*1*	*1*
Butter	*1 oz.*	*25 g.*	*2 tbsp.*
Oil	*1 tbsp.*	*15 ml.*	*1 tbsp.*
Chicken livers	*12 oz.*	*350 g.*	*12 oz.*
Salt and freshly ground pepper			
Ground mace			
Brandy	*1 tbsp.*	*1 tbsp.*	*1 tbsp.*

Chop the onion finely and crush the garlic. Put the onion, garlic, butter and oil into a bowl and cook in the microwave oven for 3 minutes, stirring once. Add the chicken livers and continue cooking for 4 minutes, stirring twice. Cool for 5 minutes and season with salt, pepper and a generous pinch of ground mace. Add the brandy and stir well. Put through a sieve or blend in a liquidiser. Press into a serving dish or individual dishes and smooth the top. Garnish with a thin slice of lemon or cucumber, or cover the top of the pâté with a little melted butter. Serve cold with toast.

SPECIAL INSTRUCTIONS
Freeze without garnish.

THAW
At room temperature 3 hours

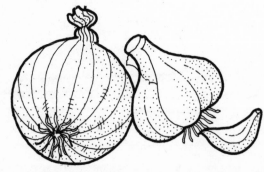

Kipper Pâté

✳ 2 months   Serves 4

INGREDIENTS	Imperial	Metric	American
Frozen kipper fillets	6 oz.	150 g.	6 oz.
Butter	1 oz.	25 g.	1 oz.
Lemon juice	2 tsp.	10 ml.	2 tsp.
Garlic clove	1	1	1
Brandy	1 tbsp.	15 ml.	1 tbsp.
Tabasco sauce	Few drops	Few drops	Few drops
Single cream	2 tbsp.	30 ml.	2 tbsp.
Lemon	½	½	½

Cut the corner of the boil-in-bag containing the kipper fillets, so that steam will escape. Put the bag on a plate and cook in the microwave oven for 5 minutes. Remove the fillets and take off any dark skin. Press through a sieve or put into a liquidiser. Add lemon juice, crushed garlic, brandy, Tabasco sauce and cream, and mix or blend until smooth. Press into a serving dish or individual dishes. Garnish with thin slices of lemon, or cover with a thin layer of melted butter. Chill and serve with hot toast.

SPECIAL INSTRUCTIONS
Freeze without garnish.

THAW
At room temperature 3 hours

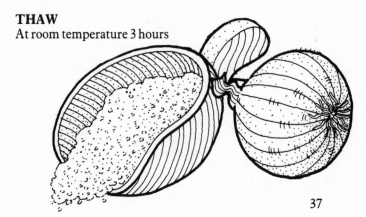

Golden Grapefruit

Serves 4

INGREDIENTS	Imperial	Metric	American
Grapefruit	2	2	2
Medium sherry	1 tbsp.	1 tbsp.	1 tbsp.
Dark soft brown sugar	4 tsp.	4 tsp.	4 tsp.
Butter	2 tsp.	2 tsp.	2 tsp.

Cut the grapefruit in halves and remove pips. Cut carefully round segments with a sharp knife to loosen them. Sprinkle with sherry and sugar and leave to stand for 30 minutes. Cut the butter in small flakes and dot on top of each grapefruit half. Heat in the microwave oven for 3 minutes. The grapefruit may be garnished with a fresh mint leaf or glacé cherry.

SPECIAL INSTRUCTIONS
Do not freeze.

Smoked Haddock Pâté

* 2 months   Serves 4

INGREDIENTS	Imperial	Metric	American
Frozen smoked haddock fillets	*6 oz.*	*150 g.*	*6 oz.*
Butter	*3 oz.*	*75 g.*	*6 tbsp.*
Plain flour	*1 oz.*	*25 g.*	*2 tbsp.*
Milk	*½ pt.*	*300 ml.*	*1¼ cups*
Single cream	*2 tbsp.*	*30 ml.*	*2 tbsp.*
Dry sherry	*1 tbsp.*	*15 ml.*	*1 tbsp.*
Salt and freshly ground black pepper			

Cut the corner of the boil-in-bag containing the haddock fillets, so that steam will escape. Put the bag on a plate and cook in the microwave oven for 5 minutes. Remove any skin from the fish and break the flesh into flakes. Put 1 oz./25 g./2 tablespoons butter in a bowl in the microwave oven and melt for 1 minute. Stir in the flour and then the milk and whisk well. Cook in the microwave oven for 4 minutes, whisking the sauce three times during cooking. Put the fish into a blender and add the sauce, remaining butter, cream, sherry and seasoning. Blend until smooth and creamy. Pour into a serving dish or individual dishes. Garnish with thin slices of cucumber or a few prawns. Chill before serving with hot toast and butter.

SPECIAL INSTRUCTIONS
Freeze without garnish.

THAW
At room temperature 3 hours

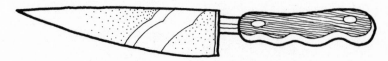

FISH AND SHELLFISH

Southern Cod

✻ 1 month   Serves 4

INGREDIENTS	Imperial	Metric	American
Cod fillets	1 lb.	450 g.	1 lb.
Oil	1 tbsp.	15 ml.	1 tbsp.
Onion	1 medium	1 medium	1 medium
Garlic clove	1	1	1
Tomatoes	2	2	2
Salt and pepper			
Sprig of basil			
Dry white wine	1/4 pt.	150 ml.	2/3 cup
Black olives	2 oz.	50 g.	1/2 cup
Chopped fresh parsley	1 tbsp.	1 tbsp.	1 tbsp.

Remove skin from the cod and cut the flesh in
1 in./2.5 cm. cubes. Put into a casserole with the oil. Chop
the onion finely and crush the garlic, and put into the
casserole. Cover and cook in the microwave oven for 3
minutes, stirring twice. Skin the tomatoes and cut them in
thick slices. Arrange on top of the fish and season with salt
and pepper. Add the basil and wine. Cover and cook for 2
minutes. Stone the olives and add to the casserole.
Microwave for 1 minute. Sprinkle with chopped parsley
before serving.

SPECIAL INSTRUCTIONS
Freeze without olives or parsley. Stir in just before
serving.

REHEAT
15 minutes

Kedgeree

* 1 month   Serves 4

INGREDIENTS	Imperial	Metric	American
Smoked haddock fillets	*1 lb.*	*450 g.*	*1 lb.*
Boiling water	*1 pt.*	*600 ml.*	*2½ cups*
Butter	*1 oz.*	*25 g.*	*2 tbsp.*
Onion	*1 medium*	*1 medium*	*1 medium*
Long grain rice	*6 oz.*	*150 g.*	*¾ cup*
Bay leaf	*1*	*1*	*1*
Salt and freshly ground pepper			
Garnish			
Hard-boiled eggs	*3*	*3*	*3*
Chopped fresh parsley	*1 tbsp.*	*1 tbsp.*	*1 tbsp.*
Butter	*2 oz.*	*50 g.*	*4 tbsp.*

Put the haddock into a shallow dish and cover with the boiling water. Cook in the microwave oven for 5 minutes. Reserve the cooking liquid. Take any skin from the fish, and flake the flesh. Put the butter into a casserole dish and heat in the microwave oven for 1 minute. Add the finely chopped onion and microwave for 2 minutes. Add the rice and bay leaf and pour on the cooking liquid. Cook for 15 minutes, stirring twice, until the liquid has been absorbed. Take out and discard the bay leaf. Stir in the fish, and season well. Chop the hard-boiled eggs and stir into the rice with the parsley and butter cut into small flakes. Microwave for 1 minute and serve at once.

SPECIAL INSTRUCTIONS
Freeze without garnish. Stir in after reheating.

REHEAT
20 minutes

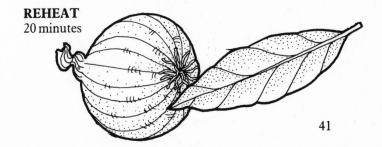

41

Poached Salmon

✳ 1 month   Serves 4

INGREDIENTS

	Imperial	Metric	American
Salmon steaks	4 × 6 oz.	4 × 150 g.	4 × 6 oz.
Water	¼ pt.	150 ml.	⅔ cup
Lemon juice	1 tbsp.	1 tbsp.	1 tbsp.
Pinch of salt			
Thin slices of cucumber and lemon to to garnish			

Place the salmon steaks in a shallow dish. Pour over the water and lemon juice and add the salt. Cover with clingfilm and make two small holes in the film. Cook in the microwave oven 7 minutes. Take out of the oven and leave to stand in the liquid for 5 minutes. Lift on to serving dish, draining well, and serve hot or cold with Hollandaise sauce or mayonnaise. Garnish with lemon and cucumber slices.

THAW
At room temperature 3 hours

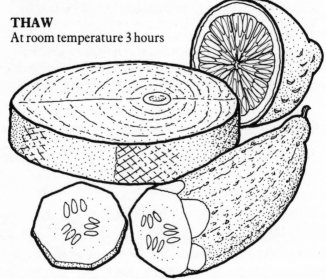

Stuffed Plaice in Wine Sauce

❋ 1 month   Serves 4

INGREDIENTS	Imperial	Metric	American
Plaice fillets (flounder)	8	8	8
Potted shrimps in butter	4 oz.	100 g.	1/2 cup
Dry white wine	1/4 pt.	150 ml.	2/3 cup
Water	1/4 pt.	150 ml.	2/3 cup
Lemon juice	1/2 tsp.	1/2 tsp.	1/2 tsp.
Bay leaf	1	1	1
Blade of mace	1	1	1
Salt and pepper			
Butter	1/2 oz.	15 g.	1 tbsp.
Plain flour	1/2 oz.	15 g.	1 tbsp.
Sprigs of watercress to garnish			

Skin the fish fillets. Divide the potted shrimps into eight portions and place one portion on each piece of fish. Roll up the fillets and place close together in a shallow dish. Mix together the wine, water and lemon juice and pour over the fish. Add the bay leaf, mace, salt and pepper. Cover with clingfilm and make two small holes in the film. Cook in the microwave oven for 5 minutes. Drain off the cooking liquid and reserve. Remove the bay leaf and mace, and keep the fish hot. Mix the butter and flour together in a bowl and pour in the cooking liquid, whisking well. Microwave for 1 minute, stir well and cook for 1 minute. Pour over the fish and garnish with watercress sprigs.

SPECIAL INSTRUCTIONS
Freeze without watercress, and add after reheating.

REHEAT
15 minutes

Trout with Almonds

✳ 1 month   Serves 4

INGREDIENTS	Imperial	Metric	American
Trout	*4 × 8 oz.*	*4 × 225 g.*	*4 × 8 oz.*
Butter	*3 oz.*	*75 g.*	*6 tbsp.*
Flaked blanched almonds	*2 oz.*	*50 g.*	*½ cup*
Salt and pepper			
Lemon juice	*1½ tsp.*	*1½ tsp.*	*1½ tsp.*
Lemon	*1*	*1*	*1*
Watercress or parsley *to garnish*			

Clean the trout and arrange in a shallow dish. Put 2 oz./50 g./4 tablespoons butter into a bowl and heat in the microwave oven for 30 seconds. Add the almonds and heat for 3 minutes until lightly coloured. Keep on one side. Sprinkle the trout with salt, pepper and lemon juice, and put a piece of the remaining butter on each one. Cover with clingfilm and make two small holes in the film. Cook in the microwave oven for 9 minutes. Spoon over the almonds and microwave for 2 minutes. Leave to stand for 2 minutes before serving. Cut lemon into four wedges and serve one with each trout. Garnish with watercress or parsley.

REHEAT
25 minutes

Baked Crab

✳ 1 month   Serves 4

INGREDIENTS	Imperial	Metric	American
Butter	1 oz.	25 g.	2 tbsp.
Onion	1 small	1 small	1 small
Dry sherry	2 tbsp.	30 ml.	2 tbsp.
Crabmeat (brown and white)	8 oz.	225 g.	8 oz.
Fresh white breadcrumbs	½ oz.	15 g.	¼ cup
Made mustard	½ tsp.	½ tsp.	½ tsp.
Worcestershire sauce	½ tsp.	½ tsp.	½ tsp.
Chopped fresh parsley	1 tbsp.	1 tbsp.	1 tbsp.
Salt and freshly ground black pepper			
Browned breadcrumbs	1 oz.	25 g.	½ cup
Grated Parmesan cheese	1 tbsp.	1 tbsp.	1 tbsp.
Lemon	1	1	1

Put the butter into a shallow dish and add the finely chopped onion. Microwave for 2 minutes. Stir in the sherry and microwave for 1 minute. Add the crabmeat, breadcrumbs, mustard, Worcestershire sauce, parsley and seasoning. Cook in the microwave oven for 3 minutes. Mix the browned breadcrumbs and cheese together and sprinkle on top of the crab. Microwave for 2 minutes. Serve immediately, garnished with lemon cut into wedges.

SPECIAL INSTRUCTIONS
Freeze without breadcrumbs and cheese topping. Add before reheating.

REHEAT
10 minutes

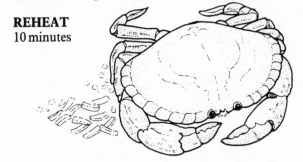

Spicy Prawns

Serves 4

INGREDIENTS

	Imperial	Metric	American
Prawns	1 lb.	450 g.	1 lb.
Oil	4 tbsp.	60 ml.	4 tbsp.
Tomato purée	1½ tbsp.	20 ml.	1½ tbsp.
Paprika	1 tsp.	1 tsp.	1 tsp.
Lemon juice	2 tbsp.	30 ml.	2 tbsp.
Coriander	½ tsp.	½ tsp.	½ tsp.
Ground cumin	½ tsp.	½ tsp.	½ tsp.
Sweet basil	½ tsp.	½ tsp.	½ tsp.
Few drops tabasco			

Thaw prawns or use fresh ones. Mix all ingredients together and pour over the prawns. Stir well and allow to stand for 5 minutes. Cover and cook in the microwave on high for 3–4 minutes. Allow to sit and cook for a further 2 minutes.

Serve hot as a starter for 6 or as a main course for 4.

SPECIAL INSTRUCTIONS
Do not freeze.

Scrambled Eggs with Prawns

Serves 2

INGREDIENTS	Imperial	Metric	American
Eggs	2	2	2
Milk	2 tbsp.	30 ml.	2 tbsp.
Butter	½ oz.	15 g.	1 tbsp.
Frozen prawns	1 oz.	25 g.	1 oz.
Freshly ground black pepper			

Break the eggs into a large mixing bowl, whisk well with the milk. Add the butter, cut into small pieces, and the prawns.

Microwave on high for one minute, then whisk again to mix the cooked and uncooked egg. Microwave on high for 1 minute and whisk again. Leave to stand for 2 minutes. This gives a soft fluffy scrambled egg mixture. For firmer eggs, cook for an extra minute and then stand for 2 minutes.

This can also be made with strips of ham added or strips of smoked salmon.

SPECIAL INSTRUCTIONS
Do not freeze.

MEAT

N.B. Although some meat dishes will look different from those cooked by other methods, their texture and flavour will not be affected in any way.

Pitta Pockets

✳ 2 months   Serves 4

INGREDIENTS	Imperial	Metric	American
Butter	1 oz.	25 g.	2 tbsp.
Onion	1 medium	1 medium	1 medium
Raw minced beef	8 oz.	25 g.	8 oz.
Garlic clove	1	1	1
Canned tomatoes	4 oz.	100 g.	4 oz.
Paprika	1 tsp.	1 tsp.	1 tsp.
Worcestershire sauce	1 tsp.	1 tsp.	1 tsp.
Chopped fresh parsley	2 tsp.	2 tsp.	2 tsp.
Salt and pepper			
Pitta breads	4	4	4

Put the butter into a shallow dish. Chop the onion finely. Add to the butter and cook in the microwave oven for 3 minutes. Add the beef and continue cooking for 5 minutes, stirring twice. Add the crushed garlic, tomatoes and their juice, paprika, Worcestershire sauce, parsley, salt and pepper. Cover and microwave for 2 minutes. Leave to stand while preparing the bread. Wrap each pitta bread in greaseproof paper and microwave for 20 seconds. Fill each pitta bread pocket with some of the meat mixture and serve at once with salad.

SPECIAL INSTRUCTIONS
Freeze meat filling only. Heat pitta bread as instructed and fill with hot meat.

REHEAT
8 minutes

Burgundy Beef

✳ 2 months   Serves 4

INGREDIENTS	Imperial	Metric	American
Streaky bacon rashers	4	4	4
Onion	1 medium	1 medium	1 medium
Chuck steak	1 lb.	450 g.	1 lb.
Beef stock	1/2 pt.	300 ml.	1 1/4 cups
Red wine	1/4 pt.	150 ml.	2/3 cup
Sprig of parsley			
Sprig of thyme			
Bay leaf	1	1	1
Garlic clove	1	1	1
Salt and freshly ground black pepper			
Button onions	8	8	8
Button mushrooms	4 oz.	100 g.	4 oz.
Chopped fresh parsley	1 tbsp.	1 tbsp.	1 tbsp.

Remove the rind from the bacon and cut into small strips. Chop the onion finely. Put bacon and onion into a casserole dish and cook in the microwave oven for 4 minutes, stirring twice. Cut the steak into cubes and add to the casserole dish. Microwave for 2 minutes. Add the stock, wine, herbs, crushed garlic, salt and pepper. Microwave for 10 minutes, stirring once. Peel the button onions and leave whole. Add to the meat and continue cooking for 20 minutes, stirring twice. Add the mushrooms, stir well and cook for 5 minutes. Leave to stand for 5 minutes before stirring, and garnish with chopped parsley.

SPECIAL INSTRUCTIONS
Freeze without parsley. Garnish after reheating.

REHEAT
20 minutes

Meat Balls in Tomato Sauce

✳ 2 months   Serves 4

INGREDIENTS	Imperial	Metric	American
Onion	1 medium	1 medium	1 medium
Butter	2 oz.	50 g.	4 tbsp.
Raw minced beef	1 lb.	450 g.	1 lb.
Fresh white breadcrumbs	1 oz.	25 g.	½ cup
Mixed herbs	½ tsp.	½ tsp.	½ tsp.
Egg	1	1	1
Salt and pepper			
Plain flour	1 oz.	25 g.	2 tbsp.
Concentrated tomato purée	2 tbsp.	2 tbsp.	2 tbsp.
Canned tomatoes	8 oz.	225 g.	8 oz.
Beef stock	½ pt.	300 ml.	1¼ cups

Chop the onion very finely. Put 1 oz./25 g./2 tablespoons butter into a shallow dish and microwave for 2 minutes. Add the onion to the butter with the beef, breadcrumbs, herbs, egg, salt and pepper. Stir well and then shape into 16 balls. Put the remaining butter into the dish and melt in the microwave oven for 1 minute. Arrange the meatballs in the butter and turn them so that they are coated in fat. Microwave for 5 minutes, turning the meatballs once. Lift out the meatballs and keep on one side. Work the flour into the fat and then mix in the tomato purée. Put the tomatoes and their juice through a sieve to get rid of the pips. Stir into the flour. Add the beef stock. Return to microwave and cook for 3 minutes, stirring twice. Add the meatballs, stir well and microwave for 8 minutes, turning the meatballs four times. Serve with pasta, rice or mashed potatoes.

REHEAT
20 minutes

Gingered Lamb Chops

❋ 2 months   Serves 4

INGREDIENTS	Imperial	Metric	American
Lamb chump chops	4	4	4
Butter	2 oz.	50 g.	4 tbsp.
Lemon juice	1 tbsp.	15 ml.	1 tbsp.
Grated lemon rind	2 tsp.	2 tsp.	2 tsp.
Ground ginger	1 tsp.	1 tsp.	1 tsp.
Garlic clove	½	½	½
Salt and pepper			

Put the chops into a shallow dish. Put the butter into a bowl and melt in the microwave oven for 1 minute. Add the lemon juice and rind, ginger, crushed garlic and seasoning and mix well. Spread on both sides of the chops. Cook in the microwave oven for 12 minutes, turning the chops three times during cooking. Serve with vegetables or a salad.

REHEAT
10 minutes

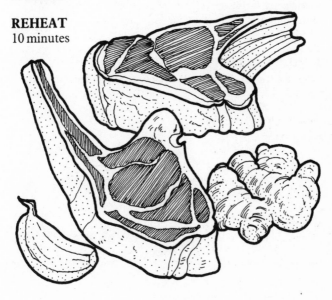

Pork in Cider Sauce

✳ 2 months   Serves 4

INGREDIENTS	Imperial	Metric	American
Butter	*1 oz.*	*25 g.*	*2 tbsp.*
Onion	*1 medium*	*1 medium*	*1 medium*
Pork tenderloin	*1 lb.*	*450 g.*	*1 lb.*
Mixed herbs	*½ tsp.*	*½ tsp.*	*½ tsp.*
Button mushrooms	*4 oz.*	*100 g.*	*4 oz.*
Dry cider	*¼ pt.*	*150 ml.*	*⅔ cup*
Salt and pepper			
Single cream	*¼ pt.*	*150 ml.*	*⅔ cup*
Chopped fresh parsley	*1 tbsp.*	*1 tbsp.*	*1 tbsp.*

Put the butter into a casserole dish. Add the finely chopped onion and cook in the microwave oven for 4 minutes. Cut the tenderloin across in thin rounds and add to the dish. Microwave for 2 minutes, stirring once. Add the herbs, sliced mushrooms, cider, salt and pepper. Cook in the microwave oven for 7 minutes, stirring twice. Stir in the cream and microwave for 2 minutes, stirring once. Sprinkle with chopped parsley before serving.

SPECIAL INSTRUCTIONS
Freeze without cream and parsley. Add just before serving.

REHEAT
15 minutes

Sausage and Apple Bake

✳ 1 month Serves 4

INGREDIENTS	Imperial	Metric	American
Pork sausages	*1 lb.*	*450 g.*	*1 lb.*
Onions	*2 large*	*2 large*	*2 large*
Eating apples	*2*	*2*	*2*
Barbecue Sauce			
(see page 87)			

Put the sausages into a shallow dish and prick well. Cover with clingfilm and make two small holes in the film. Cook in the microwave oven for 6 minutes. Take out the sausages and keep warm. Slice the onions thinly and put into the sausage fat. Cover and cook for 6 minutes. Peel the apples and cut into thin slices. Add the sausages and apples to the onions and heat for 3 minutes. Pour on the sauce and continue cooking for 4 minutes. Serve with hot crusty bread and green salad.

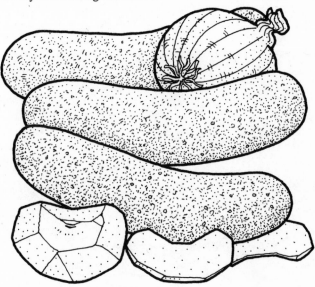

53

Apple Gammon

✳ 1 month   Serves 4

INGREDIENTS	Imperial	Metric	American
Gammon steaks	*4 × 6 oz.*	*4 × 175 g.*	*4 × 6 oz.*
Onion	*1 medium*	*1 medium*	*1 medium*
Dry cider	*½ pt.*	*300 ml.*	*1¼ cups*
Eating apple	*1*	*1*	*1*
Sage leaves	*2*	*2*	*2*
Salt and pepper			

Remove the rind from the gammon steaks. Put the steaks in a casserole in a single layer and cook in the microwave oven for 6 minutes, turning once. Chop the onion finely and add to the dish. Microwave for 3 minutes. Add the cider. Peel and core the apple and cut in thin slices. Add to the dish with the finely chopped sage leaves, salt and pepper. Microwave for 7 minutes, stirring twice. Leave to stand for 5 minutes before serving.

REHEAT
20 minutes

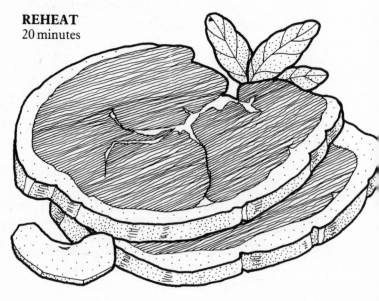

Herbed Liver

✻ 2 months   Serves 4

INGREDIENTS	Imperial	Metric	American
Lambs' liver	*12 oz.*	*350 g.*	*12 oz.*
Onion	*1 medium*	*1 medium*	*1 medium*
Streaky bacon rashers	*2*	*2*	*2*
Butter	*1 oz.*	*25 g.*	*2 tbsp.*
Oil	*1 tbsp.*	*15 ml.*	*1 tbsp.*
Canned tomatoes	*1 lb.*	*450 g.*	*1 lb.*
Mixed herbs	*½ tsp.*	*½ tsp.*	*½ tsp.*
Salt and pepper			

Cut the liver in thin slices. Chop the onion and bacon.
Put the butter and oil in a casserole and heat in the
microwave oven for 2 minutes. Add the onion and bacon
and continue cooking for 3 minutes, stirring once. Add
the liver and cook for 1 minute. Sieve the tomatoes to get
rid of the pips. Pour over the liver and stir in the herbs and
seasoning. Continue cooking for 7 minutes, stirring twice.
Leave to stand for 5 minutes before serving.

REHEAT
15 minutes

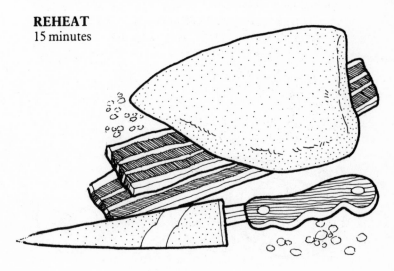

Kidneys in Red Wine

✳ 2 months   Serves 4

INGREDIENTS	Imperial	Metric	American
Onion	1 small	1 small	1 small
Button mushrooms	4 oz.	100 g.	4 oz.
Butter	1½ oz.	40 g.	3 tbsp.
Lambs' kidneys	10	10	10
Plain flour	½ oz.	15 g.	1 tbsp.
Red wine	¼ pt.	150 ml.	⅔ cup
Beef stock	4 tbsp.	60 ml.	4 tbsp.
Made mustard	1 tsp.	1 tsp.	1 tsp.
Salt and pepper			
Chopped fresh parsley	1 tbsp.	1 tbsp.	1 tbsp.

Chop the onion finely and slice the mushrooms. Put the onion and butter into a shallow dish and cook in the microwave oven for 4 minutes, stirring once. Add the mushrooms, and cook for 1 minute. Skin the kidneys, cut them in half lengthwise. Cut out the white core from each half. Add to the onion and cook for 5 minutes, stirring once. Stir in the flour, and then the wine, stock and mustard, and season with salt and pepper. Mix well and microwave for 8 minutes. Leave to stand for 5 minutes. Serve sprinkled with parsley.

REHEAT
15 minutes

SPECIAL INSTRUCTIONS
Freeze without parsley. Garnish after reheating.

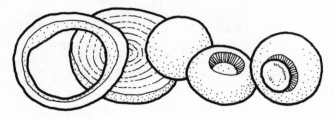

Mushroom Stuffed Steaks

Serves 2

INGREDIENTS	Imperial	Metric	American
2 thick cut sirloin steaks each weighing 6–8 oz./150–225 g.			
Mushrooms	*2 oz.*	*50 g.*	*2 oz.*
Fresh herbs, finely chopped	*1 tbsp.*	*1 tbsp.*	*1 tbsp.*
Butter	*1 oz.*	*25 g.*	*2 tbsp.*
Freshly ground black pepper			

Preheat browning dish for 8 minutes.

Use a sharp knife to cut a slit in the side of the steaks so there is room for the stuffing. Chop the mushrooms finely, add the herbs and season well. Cut the butter into small pieces and stir in. Divide the filling between the steaks. Lay the steaks in the hot browning dish, press down well and turn once. When they stop sizzling return to the microwave and cook uncovered for 3–5 minutes. Check after 3 minutes by lifting the top section of meat, so that you can see the pink inside. Cook according to taste.

SPECIAL INSTRUCTIONS
Do not freeze.

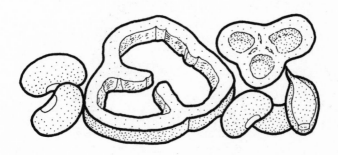

Lamb and Potato Casserole

*   2–3 months   Serves 2

INGREDIENTS	Imperial	Metric	American
4 chump chops total weight			
1 lb./450 g.			
Stock	*6 tbsp.*	*90 ml.*	*6 tbsp.*
Rosemary, dried	*½ tsp.*	*½ tsp.*	*½ tsp.*
Potatoes	*2*	*2*	*2*
Butter	*½ oz.*	*15 g.*	*1 tbsp.*
Freshly ground black			
pepper			

Preheat browning dish for 8 minutes. Sear the chops, turning once. Pour the stock around the chops and add the rosemary. Slice potatoes very thinly and arrange overlapping slices on top of the lamb. Cut the butter in small pieces, sprinkle on top. Add plenty of freshly ground black pepper. Put the lid on the dish and cook in the microwave for 6 minutes on high. Check how soft the potatoes are and cook for a further 2 minutes if necessary. This will depend on the type of potatoes used and how thinly sliced they are.

REHEAT
Defrost on low for 5 minutes. Stand for 3 minutes. Reheat on high for 4 minutes.

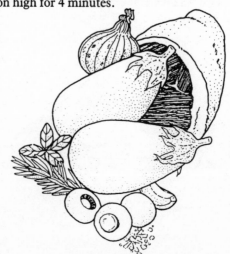

Veal Stroganoff

Serves 4

INGREDIENTS	Imperial	Metric	American
Veal, cut into cubes	*1 lb.*	*450 g.*	*1 lb.*
Mushrooms	*4 oz.*	*100 g.*	*¼ lb.*
Butter	*1 oz.*	*25 g.*	*2 tbsp.*
Can of sweet red peppers	*6½ oz.*	*185 g.*	*small can*
Carton soured cream	*5 fl. oz.*	*145 ml.*	*⅔ cup*
French mustard	*½ tsp.*	*½ tsp.*	*½ tsp.*
Freshly ground black pepper			

Preheat browning dish for 8 minutes. Once hot add the meat cubes and turn well to brown the outside slightly. Remove from browning dish. Slice the mushrooms thinly. Melt the butter in the browning dish, add the mushrooms, stir well and cook for 2 minutes.

Drain the oil from the sweet peppers and cut into thin strips. Add the meat and peppers to the mushrooms. Cover with cling film, make 2 slits in the top and microwave for 3 minutes. Stir well and cook for a further 2 minutes.

Stir the mustard into the soured cream and add plenty of freshly ground pepper. Add to the meat and stir in well. Cover and return to the microwave and cook for 3 minutes. Serve hot with rice.

SPECIAL INSTRUCTIONS
Do not freeze.

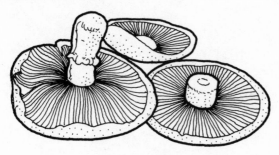

Bacon Steaks with Orange Sauce

✳ 1 month   Serves 2

INGREDIENTS	Imperial	Metric	American
4 loin bacon steaks, total weight 8–10 oz./225–300 g.			
Orange juice	1 tbsp.	15 ml.	1 tbsp.
Honey	1 tsp.	1 tsp.	1 tsp.
Cornflour	½ tsp.	½ tsp.	½ tsp.
Freshly ground black pepper			

Preheat browning dish for 8 minutes. Add bacon steaks, pressing down well and turning once to brown them. Mix the honey, cornflour and orange juice together and pour over the steaks. Add plenty of freshly ground black pepper. Microwave on high uncovered for 3–4 minutes. Serve hot.

REHEAT
Defrost on low for 3 minutes. Reheat on high for 2–3 minutes.

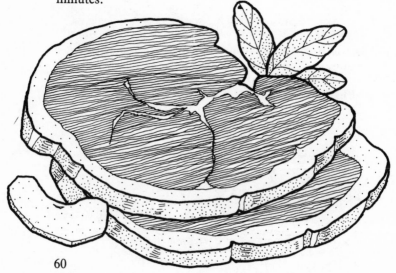

Sunday Brunch

Serves 2

INGREDIENTS	Imperial	Metric	American
Chipolata sausages	4	4	4
Tomatoes	2	2	2
Streaky bacon	2 rashers	2 rashers	2 rashers
Bread	2 slices	2 slices	2 slices
Butter	1½ oz.	35 g.	3 tbsp.
Eggs	2	2	2
Salt and pepper			

Preheat browning dish for 8 minutes. Add sausages, and roll them over, pressing down to brown them. Cut tomatoes in half. Season well and put a small knob of butter on top of each. Add to the browning dish. Return to the oven and cook for 2–3 minutes. Remove and place food on a warm serving dish and cover. Wipe round the browning dish. Melt the rest of the butter.

Lay the slices of bacon between two sheets of kitchen towel, and cook for 2–3 minutes. Remove and add to the sausages.

Reheat browning dish for 5–6 minutes. Brush each slice of bread with the melted butter, on both sides. Cut a hole in each using a biscuit cutter. Once the dish is hot, lay the bread in to brown. Press down well and turn over once. Brown the cut out circle of bread too. Break an egg into the hole in the bread, and pierce the yolk with a cocktail stick to prevent it exploding. It may be necessary to cook 1 slice at a time, depending on the size of the browning dish. 1 slice takes approximately 1½ minutes, 2 slices about 2½ minutes. Serve, with the cut out circle on top, with the sausages, bacon and tomatoes.

SPECIAL INSTRUCTIONS
Do not freeze.

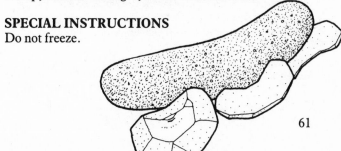

61

POULTRY

N.B. Although some poultry dishes will look different from those cooked by other methods, their texture and flavour will not be affected in any way.

Italian Chicken

✳ 2 months   Serves 4

INGREDIENTS	Imperial	Metric	American
Chicken joints	*4*	*4*	*4*
Onion	*1 small*	*1 small*	*1 small*
Garlic clove	*1*	*1*	*1*
Oil	*1 tbsp.*	*15 ml.*	*1 tbsp.*
Canned tomatoes	*1 lb.*	*450 g.*	*1 lb.*
Concentrated tomato purée	*4 tbsp.*	*4 tbsp.*	*4 tbsp.*
Sugar	*1 tsp.*	*1 tsp.*	*1 tsp.*
Fresh marjoram	*1 tsp.*	*1 tsp.*	*1 tsp.*
Fresh thyme	*½ tsp.*	*½ tsp.*	*½ tsp.*
Chopped fresh parsley	*2 tsp.*	*2 tsp.*	*2 tsp.*
Red wine	*¼ pt.*	*150 ml.*	*⅔ cup*
Salt and pepper			
Button mushrooms	*4 oz.*	*100 g.*	*4 oz.*

Chop the onion finely and crush the garlic. Put into a casserole dish with the oil and cook in the microwave oven for 4 minutes, stirring twice. Add the tomatoes and their juice, purée, sugar, herbs, wine, salt and pepper. Add the chicken pieces and make sure that they are covered with the other ingredients. Cover and cook in the microwave oven for 20 minutes. Slice the mushrooms and stir into the casserole. Microwave for 10 minutes without a cover, stirring the sauce twice. Cover and leave to stand for 10 minutes before serving with rice or pasta.

REHEAT
15 minutes

Indian Chicken

✳ 2 months   Serves 4

INGREDIENTS	Imperial	Metric	American
Chicken breasts	4	4	4
Natural yoghurt	1/4 pt.	150 ml.	2/3 cup
Curry powder	1–2 tsp.	1–2 tsp.	1–2 tsp.
Ground ginger	1–2 tsp.	1–2 tsp.	1–2 tsp.
Ground cinnamon	1/2–1 tsp.	1/2–1 tsp.	1/2–1 tsp.
Garlic clove	1/2	1/2	1/2
Lemon juice	2 tsp.	2 tsp.	2 tsp.
Salt and pepper			

Remove skin from the chicken. Using a sharp knife, make slashes at 1 in./2.5 cm. intervals on the breasts. Mix the yoghurt with the curry powder, ginger, cinnamon, crushed garlic, lemon juice, salt and pepper. Spread all over the chicken, pressing down well. Cover with clingfilm and leave in the refrigerator for at least 2 hours. Put the chicken breasts into a shallow dish with any of the mixture which has run off them. Cook in the microwave oven for 5 minutes. Turn over the chicken breasts and microwave for 10 minutes, turning the chicken once more. Serve with rice and chutney.

REHEAT
15 minutes

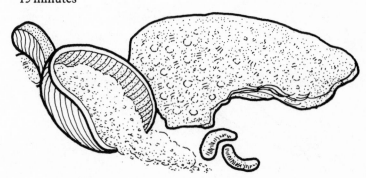

Herbed Chicken Drumsticks

* 2 months   Serves 4

INGREDIENTS	Imperial	Metric	American
Chicken drumsticks	8	8	8
Butter	4 oz.	100 g.	½ cup
Tarragon	1 tsp.	1 tsp.	1 tsp.
Chives	2 tsp.	2 tsp.	2 tsp.
Parsley	2 tbsp.	2 tbsp.	2 tbsp.
Salt and freshly ground black pepper			

Put the butter into a shallow dish and heat in the microwave oven for 1 minute. Add chopped herbs, salt and pepper, and mix well. Put in the drumsticks and coat them thoroughly in the butter. Cook in the microwave oven for 16 minutes, turning the drumsticks three times during cooking. Serve hot or cold with vegetables or salad.

THAW
At room temperature 3 hours
OR
REHEAT
20 minutes, turning three times

Turkey Bake

✳ 2 months   Serves 4

INGREDIENTS	Imperial	Metric	American
Boneless turkey (or chicken) breasts	1 lb.	450 g.	1 lb.
Onion	1 medium	1 medium	1 medium
Oil	2 tbsp.	30 ml.	2 tbsp.
Plain flour	1 oz.	25 g.	2 tbsp.
Medium dry cider	¾ pt.	450 ml.	2 cups
Salt and pepper			
Canned red peppers	4 oz.	100 g.	4 oz.
Dry sherry	2 tbsp.	30 ml.	2 tbsp.
Double cream	2 tbsp.	30 ml.	2 tbsp.

Cut the turkey or chicken breasts into cubes. Chop the onion finely and put into a casserole dish with the oil. Heat in the microwave oven for 3 minutes. Stir in the pieces of turkey or chicken and cook for 5 minutes, stirring twice. Stir in the flour, mixing well. Microwave for 1 minute. Stir in the cider, mixing well until smooth, and season with salt and pepper. Cook in the microwave oven for 5 minutes, stirring twice. Cut the red peppers into strips and stir into the mixture. Microwave for 3 minutes, stirring once. Stir in the sherry and cream and serve at once with rice or pasta.

SPECIAL INSTRUCTIONS
Freeze without cream. Stir in after reheating.

REHEAT
15 minutes

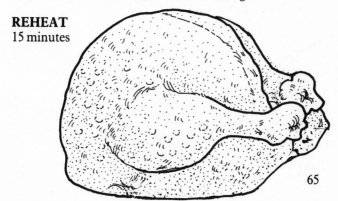

Herbed Chicken Livers

✳ 1 month   Serves 4

INGREDIENTS	Imperial	Metric	American
Chicken livers	1 lb.	450 g.	1 lb.
Oil	4 tbsp.	60 ml.	4 tbsp.
Wine vinegar	3 tbsp.	45 ml.	3 tbsp.
Salt and freshly ground black pepper			
Dried basil	1 tsp.	1 tsp.	1 tsp.
Bay leaf	1	1	1
Butter	1 oz.	25 g.	2 tbsp.
Red pepper	1	1	1
Onion	1 large	1 large	1 large

Rinse the chicken livers and dry in kitchen paper. Put into a shallow dish. Mix the oil, vinegar, salt, plenty of pepper and herbs and pour over the chicken livers. Cover with clingfilm and leave in the refrigerator for 2 hours. Put the butter into a shallow dish and heat in the microwave oven for 1 minute. Add the pepper and onion cut in thin slices and cook for 5 minutes, stirring once. Drain the liquid from the livers and reserve. Add the livers to the pepper and onion and microwave for 5 minutes, stirring once. Remove the bay leaf from the liquid, and pour the liquid over the livers. Cook for 5 minutes, stirring once. Stir well before serving. Serve on toast or with rice.

REHEAT
15 minutes

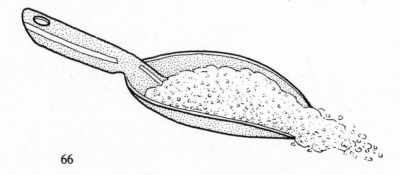

Sweet and Sour Turkey

✳ 2 months   Serves 4

INGREDIENTS	Imperial	Metric	American
Canned pineapple	1 lb.	450 g.	1 lb.
Chicken stock cube	1	1	1
Wine vinegar	3 tbsp.	45 ml.	3 tbsp.
Made mustard	1/4 tsp.	1/4 tsp.	1/4 tsp.
Soy sauce	1 tbsp.	15 ml.	1 tbsp.
Light soft brown sugar	1 oz.	25 g.	2 tbsp.
Salt and pepper			
Cooked turkey	1 1/2 lb.	675 g.	1 1/2 lb.
Green pepper	1 medium	1 medium	1 medium
Onion	1 small	1 small	1 small
Cornflour	1/2 oz.	15 g.	1 tbsp.
Maraschino cherries	2 oz.	50 g.	1/2 cup

Drain the pineapple. Mix the syrup with the crumbled stock cube, vinegar, mustard, soy sauce and sugar and season with salt and pepper. Put into a casserole dish and mix well. Heat in the microwave oven for 5 minutes. Cut the turkey in cubes. Cut the green pepper in strips and slice the onion thinly. Stir turkey, pepper and onion into the casserole. Cover and microwave for 5 minutes. Mix the cornflour with a little water and stir into the mixture. Cover and microwave for 5 minutes until the sauce is clear and thick. Stir in the pineapple chunks and cherries and mix well. Cover and leave to stand for 2 minutes. Serve with rice or noodles.

REHEAT
15 minutes

67

Chicken with Celery

Serves 4

INGREDIENTS

	Imperial	Metric	American
Chicken breasts	*4*	*4*	*4*
Sticks of celery	*2*	*2*	*2*
Carrots	*2*	*2*	*2*
Plain flour	*1 tbsp.*	*1 tbsp.*	*1 tbsp.*
Paprika	*1 tsp.*	*1 tsp.*	*1 tsp.*
Dried oregano	*1 tsp.*	*1 tsp.*	*1 tsp.*
Small can condensed asparagus soup			
Freshly ground black pepper			

Wash celery and carrots and cut into thin strips about 1 cm/½ inch long. Cut the chicken breasts across the width into short strips. Place the flour and seasonings in a plastic bag, add the chicken pieces and shake well to coat them.

Place the vegetable sticks in a large glass pie dish, and add the chicken on top. Pour the soup into a measuring jug, and add sufficient cold water to make up to ½ pt./275 ml./1¼ cups. Stir well and pour over the vegetables and chicken. Cover the dish and microwave on high for 5 minutes. Stir well, bringing the pieces of chicken from the outside of the dish to the centre. Return to the microwave and cook for 3–5 minues. Serve hot.

NB. The vegetables in this dish should remain quite crisp. If preferred, they can be precooked in the microwave for 2 minutes to give a softer result.

SPECIAL INSTRUCTIONS
Do not freeze.

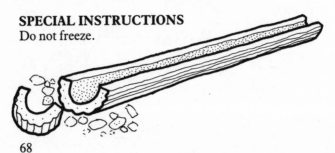

Roast Chicken

Serves 4–6

INGREDIENTS	Imperial	Metric	American
Chicken, fresh or completely thawed	3 lb.	1.5 kg.	3 lb.
Butter	2 oz.	50 g.	4 tbsp.
Lemon juice	1/2 tsp.	1/2 tsp.	1/2 tsp.
French mustard	1/2 tsp.	1/2 tsp.	1/2 tsp.
Dried mixed herbs	1 tsp.	1 tsp.	1 tsp.
Freshly ground black pepper			

Mix the butter, lemon juice, mustard and herbs together. Put half of this mixture inside the cavity of the bird. Lift the skin over the breast of the chicken and carefully slide your fingers underneath it, to loosen it from the meat. Start at the cavity and work along the breast, so that you have a loose pocket of skin. Slide the remaining butter mixture under the skin, pushing it in as far as possible. Pat it down, on top of the skin to spread it evenly.

Place an upturned saucer in a large pie dish and stand the chicken, breast down, on this. Cover with cling film, cut 2 slits in the film. Cook on high for 5 minutes, then turn the chicken the right way up. Cook on high for 10 minutes. Turn the chicken breast side down and cook for 5 minutes.

Remove from the oven, turn right way up and stand for 5 minutes before carving.

SPECIAL INSTRUCTIONS
Do not freeze.

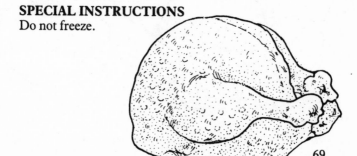

VEGETABLE DISHES

Cauliflower Cheese

Serves 4

INGREDIENTS	Imperial	Metric	American
Cauliflower	1 medium	1 medium	1 medium
Water	4 tbsp.	4 tbsp.	4 tbsp.
Cheese Sauce (see page 79–White Sauce variation)			
Grated Cheddar cheese	1 oz.	25 g.	¼ cup
Paprika			

Wash the cauliflower well and trim the green leaves. Put into a bowl with the water. Cover with clingfilm and make two small holes in the film. Cook in the microwave oven for 12 minutes. Leave to stand for 5 minutes and drain off water. Put the cauliflower into a serving dish and pour on the cheese sauce. Sprinkle with cheese and a pinch of paprika. Microwave for 3 minutes.

SPECIAL INSTRUCTIONS
Do not freeze.

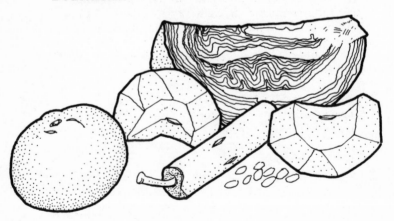

Ratatouille

✳ 2 months   Serves 4

INGREDIENTS	Imperial	Metric	American
Butter	*1 oz.*	*25 g.*	*2 tbsp.*
Oil	*2 tbsp.*	*30 ml.*	*2 tbsp.*
Onions	*2 medium*	*2 medium*	*2 medium*
Garlic clove	*1–2*	*1–2*	*1–2*
Courgettes (zucchini)	*8 oz.*	*225 g.*	*8 oz.*
Aubergines	*12 oz.*	*350 g.*	*12 oz.*
Green pepper	*1*	*1*	*1*
Tomatoes	*8 oz.*	*225 g.*	*8 oz.*
Chopped fresh parsley	*2 tbsp.*	*2 tbsp.*	*2 tbsp.*
Salt and pepper			

Put the butter and oil in a casserole and heat in the microwave oven for 2 minutes. Slice the onions thinly and crush the garlic. Add to the fat and cook for 5 minutes. Do not peel the courgettes or aubergines but slice them thinly. Remove the seeds from the green pepper and cut the flesh in thin slices. Peel the tomatoes and chop coarsely. Stir the vegetables into the onions, stir well and cover with clingfilm. Make two small holes in the film. Cook in the microwave oven for 20 minutes, stirring twice during cooking. Uncover and cook for 7 minutes. Stir in parsley and season well. Serve hot or cold, with French bread.

SPECIAL INSTRUCTIONS
Freeze without parsley. Stir in after reheating.

THAW
At room temperature 3 hours
OR
REHEAT
8 minutes

Orange Glazed Carrots

* 2 months   Serves 4

INGREDIENTS	Imperial	Metric	American
Carrots	*1 lb.*	*450 g.*	*1 lb.*
Dark soft brown sugar	*1½ oz.*	*40 g.*	*¼ cup*
Butter	*1½ oz.*	*40 g.*	*3 tbsp.*
Orange juice	*3 tbsp.*	*45 ml.*	*3 tbsp.*
Grated lemon peel	*1 tsp.*	*1 tsp.*	*1 tsp.*
Salt	*¼ tsp.*	*¼ tsp.*	*¼ tsp.*

Scrape or peel the carrots and cut them into thin slices. Put into a casserole with all the other ingredients and stir well. Cover and cook in the microwave oven for 13 minutes, stirring twice. These are particularly good served with ham.

REHEAT
10 minutes

Hot Spinach Salad

* Serves 4

INGREDIENTS	Imperial	Metric	American
Bacon rashers	*6*	*6*	*6*
Onion	*1 small*	*1 small*	*1 small*
Pepper			
Sugar	*½ oz.*	*15 g.*	*1 tbsp.*
Wine vinegar	*6 tbsp.*	*100 ml.*	*6 tbsp.*
Water	*6 tbsp.*	*100 ml.*	*6 tbsp.*
Fresh spinach	*1 lb.*	*450 g.*	*1 lb.*
Hard-boiled egg	*1*	*1*	*1*

Remove bacon rinds. Put bacon on a dish and cover with a piece of kitchen paper. Cook in microwave oven for 6 minutes until the bacon is crisp. Chop the bacon finely, and reserve any fat which has run out. Put the bacon fat into a bowl with finely chopped onion and microwave for 2½ minutes until the onion pieces are crisp. Stir in pepper, sugar, vinegar and water and microwave 2½ minutes. Meanwhile, wash the spinach and remove stems. Put the leaves into a serving bowl. Pour over hot dressing and toss with crumbled bacon and finely chopped egg.

SPECIAL INSTRUCTIONS
Do not freeze.

French Green Peas

✻ 2 months   Serves 4

INGREDIENTS	Imperial	Metric	American
Butter	*1 oz.*	*25 g.*	*2 tbsp.*
Spring onions	*4*	*4*	*4*
(scallions)			
Crisp lettuce	*1*	*1*	*1*
Frozen peas	*10 oz.*	*350 g.*	*10 oz.*
Salt and pepper			

Put the butter into a vegetable serving dish. Chop the spring onions finely. Add to the butter and cook in microwave oven for 1 minute. Shred the lettuce finely and put into the dish with the peas, salt and pepper. Cover with clingfilm, and make two small holes in the top. Microwave for 2 minutes. Remove clingfilm and continue cooking for 2 minutes. Serve immediately.

REHEAT
5 minutes

Courgettes in Tomato Sauce

✳ 2 months   Serves 4

INGREDIENTS	Imperial	Metric	American
Butter	*1 oz.*	*25 g.*	*2 tbsp.*
Oil	*2 tbsp.*	*30 ml.*	*2 tbsp.*
Courgettes (zucchini)	*1 lb.*	*450 g.*	*1 lb.*
Garlic cloves	*2*	*2*	*2*
Tomatoes	*4*	*4*	*4*
Mushrooms	*4 oz.*	*100 g.*	*1 cup*
Salt and pepper			
Chopped parsley	*1 tbsp.*	*1 tbsp.*	*1 tbsp.*

Wipe the courgettes clean but do not peel them. Cut across in ½ in./1.25 cm. slices. Put the butter and oil into a shallow dish and heat in the microwave oven for 1 minute. Stir in the courgettes and crushed garlic. Cover with clingfilm and microwave for 2 minutes. Skin the tomatoes, cut in half and discard seeds. Chop flesh roughly. Chop the mushrooms finely. Stir into the courgettes, cover and microwave again for 2 minutes. Season well, stir vegetables, cover and continue cooking for 2 minutes. Garnish with chopped parsley.

SPECIAL INSTRUCTIONS
Freeze without parsley. Sprinkle on after reheating.

REHEAT
10 minutes

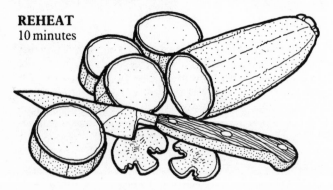

Stuffed Tomatoes

* 1 month   Serves 4

INGREDIENTS	Imperial	Metric	American
Tomatoes	4 large	4 large	4 large
Cooked ham	4 oz.	100 g.	½ cup
Onion	1 small	1 small	1 small
Fresh breadcrumbs	1 oz.	25 g.	½ cup
Button mushrooms	2 oz.	50 g.	½ cup
Grated Parmesan cheese	1 tbsp.	1 tbsp.	1 tbsp.
Chopped fresh parsley	1 tbsp.	1 tbsp.	1 tbsp.

Cut the tops from the tomatoes about 1½ ins./3.75 cm. down from the stalk. Using a small spoon, scoop out the flesh in the centre. Put this through a sieve to get rid of the pips. Chop the ham, onion and mushrooms very finely. Mix with the tomato juice and breadcrumbs. Cook in microwave oven for 2 minutes. Spoon the mixture into the tomatoes and stand them in a shallow serving dish. Microwave for 1 minute. Sprinkle with cheese, and then with parsley and serve at once.

SPECIAL INSTRUCTIONS
Freeze without cheese and parsley. Garnish after reheating.

REHEAT
5 minutes

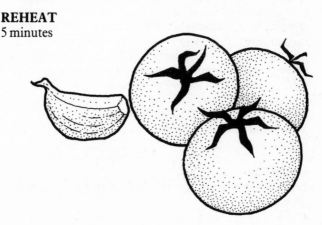

Chick Pea and Vegetable Gratin

*   2 months   Serves 4

INGREDIENTS	Imperial	Metric	American
Frozen mixed vegetables (continental ones are best)	*4 oz.*	*100 g.*	*1/4 lb.*
Cooked potatoes	*2 oz.*	*50 g.*	*2 oz.*
Can chick peas	*15 oz.*	*430 g.*	*large can*
Butter	*2 oz.*	*50 g.*	*4 tbsp.*
Wholemeal flour	*2 oz.*	*50 g.*	*1/2 cup*
Milk	*13 fl. oz.*	*350 ml.*	*1 3/4 cups*
Dry English mustard	*1/4 tsp.*	*1/4 tsp.*	*1/4 tsp.*
Grated cheese	*1 oz.*	*25 g.*	*1 oz.*
Freshly ground black pepper			
Tomatoes	*2 small*	*2 small*	*2 small*

Place the frozen vegetables, chopped potatoes and drained chick peas in a large flat dish. Cut the butter into pieces and place in a large glass mixing bowl. Add the flour and the milk. Whisk to mix the ingredients together. Microwave on high for 2 minutes. Remove and whisk well. Microwave on high for 1 minute. Remove and whisk. Microwave on high for 1 minute. Remove and whisk. The sauce should be thick and creamy. Add the mustard, cheese and pepper and stir well. Pour over the vegetables. Slice the tomatoes thinly and arrange overlapping slices around the centre of the dish. Microwave on high for 4–5 minutes.

SPECIAL INSTRUCTIONS
Serves four as a lunch. Serve with wholemeal bread or french bread.

REHEAT
Defrost on low for 5 minutes. Reheat on high for 3–4 minutes.

76

Creamed Beans and Corn

✳ 2 months   Serves 4

INGREDIENTS	Imperial	Metric	American
Broad beans	*10 oz.*	*300 g.*	*10 oz.*
Sweetcorn kernels	*10 oz.*	*300 g.*	*10 oz.*
Green or red pepper	*½*	*½*	*½*
Salt and pepper			
Pinch of sugar			
Butter	*2 oz.*	*50 g.*	*¼ cup*
Single cream	*¼ pt.*	*150 ml.*	*⅔ cup*

If frozen vegetables are used for this dish, they should be thawed before use. Drained canned sweetcorn may be used, but should not be precooked with the beans. Put beans and corn into a casserole with 2 tablespoons water. Cover and cook in microwave oven for 12 minutes. Drain off any surplus liquid. Add very finely chopped pepper, salt and pepper and a pinch of sugar and stir well. Cut the butter into thin flakes and add to the vegetables with the cream. Stir well, cover and microwave for 3 minutes.

SPECIAL INSTRUCTIONS
Freeze without cream. Stir in after reheating.

REHEAT
10 minutes

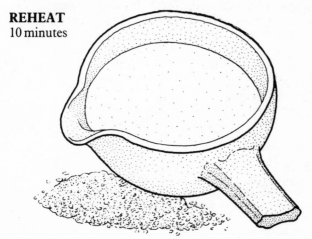

Stuffed Baked Potatoes

✳ 1 month   Serves 4

INGREDIENTS	Imperial	Metric	American
Potatoes	*4 large (6 oz. each)*	*4 large (150 g. each)*	*4 large (6 oz. each)*

Various fillings (see below)

Scrub the potatoes well and prick the skins all over with a fork. Cook in the microwave oven for 8 minutes. Turn the potatoes and continue cooking for 6 minutes. Take out of the oven and leave to stand for 5 minutes. Cut the top from each potato and scoop out the potato flesh into a bowl, leaving a 'wall' of flesh and potato skin. Mix the potato with chosen filling and refill the potatoes. Sprinkle with 1 oz./25 g./¼ cup grated Cheddar cheese and microwave for 3 minutes.

FILLINGS
Minced Beef   While the potatoes are standing, microwave 8 oz./225 g./8 oz. raw minced beef and 1 small onion, chopped finely, for 4 minutes. Mix with the potato with 1 tablespoon tomato ketchup, salt and pepper.

Smoked Fish   Cut the corner of a boil-in-the-bag containing 6 oz./150 g./6 oz. smoked haddock. Put the bag on a plate and cook in microwave oven for 5 minutes. Remove any skin from the fish and break the flesh into flakes. Mix fish with the potato, 2 oz./50 g./¼ cup butter, salt and pepper.

Ham and Cheese   Mix 4 oz./100 g./1 cup finely chopped cooked ham with 2 oz./50 g./½ cup grated Cheddar cheese, 1 oz./25 g./2 tablespoons butter, 2 teaspoons Worcestershire sauce, salt and pepper.

REHEAT
5 minutes for each potato

SAUCES

White Sauce

✳ 2 months

INGREDIENTS	Imperial	Metric	American
Butter	*1 oz.*	*25 g.*	*2 tbsp.*
Plain flour	*1 oz.*	*25 g.*	*2 tbsp.*
Milk	*½ pt.*	*300 ml.*	*1¼ cups*
Salt and pepper			

Put the butter in a bowl and melt in the microwave oven for 1 minute. Work in the flour and gradually stir in the milk. Season with salt and pepper. Cook in the microwave oven for 6 minutes, stirring three times during cooking.

Cheese sauce   After cooking, stir in 2 oz./50 g./⅓ cup grated cheese.
Egg sauce   After cooking, stir in two finely chopped hard-boiled eggs.
Onion sauce   After cooking, stir in 2 finely chopped onions cooked in butter until soft and golden.
Parsley sauce   After cooking, stir in 2 tablespoons chopped fresh parsley.
Mushroom sauce   After cooking, stir in 2 oz./50 g./½ cup finely chopped cooked mushrooms.

REHEAT
5 minutes, stirring frequently

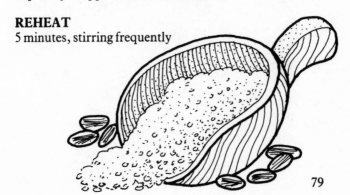

Bread Sauce

✻ 2 months

INGREDIENTS	Imperial	Metric	American
Onion	1 small	1 small	1 small
Cloves	6	6	6
Milk	½ pt.	300 ml.	1¼ cups
Fresh white breadcrumbs	3 oz.	75 g.	1½ cups
Butter	1 oz.	25 g.	2 tbsp.
Salt and pepper			
Single cream	2 tbsp.	2 tbsp.	2 tbsp.

Peel the onion and keep it whole. Stick the cloves into the onion. Put into a bowl with the milk and cook in the microwave oven for 4 minutes. Remove and discard the onion. Stir the breadcrumbs and butter into the milk and cook in the microwave for 2 minutes. Season with salt and pepper and stir in the cream. Microwave for 30 seconds and serve hot with poultry or game.

SPECIAL INSTRUCTIONS
Freeze without cream. Stir in after reheating.

REHEAT
5 minutes, stirring frequently

Tomato Sauce

✳ 2 months

INGREDIENTS	Imperial	Metric	American
Onion	1 medium	1 medium	1 medium
Garlic clove	1	1	1
Olive oil	1 tbsp.	15 ml.	1 tbsp.
Ripe tomatoes	1 lb.	450 g.	1 lb.
Salt	1 tsp.	1 tsp.	1 tsp.
Sugar	1 tsp.	1 tsp.	1 tsp.
Paprika	1 tsp.	1 tsp.	1 tsp.
Vinegar	1 tbsp.	1 tbsp.	1 tbsp.
Bay leaf	1	1	1
Pepper			

Chop the onion finely and crush the garlic. Put into a bowl with the oil and cook in the microwave oven for 4 minutes. Stir twice while cooking. Skin the tomatoes and take out and discard pips. Cut the flesh in small pieces. Add all the ingredients to the bowl and continue cooking for 7 minutes, stirring twice. Remove the bay leaf and discard. For a smooth sauce, put through a sieve or blend in a liquidiser; for use with pasta, the sauce need not be smooth. After sieving or blending, reheat in the microwave for 2 minutes. Serve with pasta, meat, fish or vegetables.

REHEAT
5 minutes

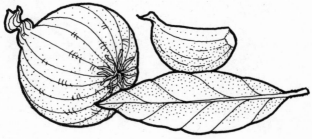

Barbecue Sauce

✳ 2 months

INGREDIENTS	Imperial	Metric	American
Onion	1 medium	1 medium	1 medium
Butter	1 oz.	25 g.	2 tbsp.
Plain flour	½ oz.	15 g.	1 tbsp.
Made mustard	2 tsp.	2 tsp.	2 tsp.
Worcestershire sauce	1 tbsp.	1 tbsp.	1 tbsp.
Tabasco sauce	1 tsp.	1 tsp.	1 tsp.
Dark soft brown sugar	½ oz.	15 g.	1 tbsp.
Salt	1 tsp.	1 tsp.	1 tsp.
Vinegar	1 tbsp.	1 tbsp.	1 tbsp.
Tomato juice	½ pt.	300 ml.	1¼ cups

Chop the onion finely. Put into a bowl with the butter and cook in the microwave oven for 4 minutes. Stir in the flour and then all the remaining ingredients. Cook in the microwave oven for 8 minutes, stirring twice during cooking. Serve hot with chicken, steak, chops, sausages or burgers.

REHEAT
5 minutes

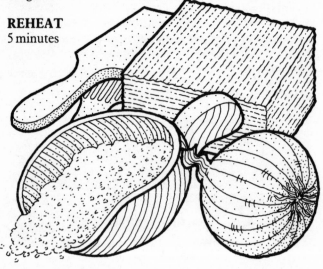

Apple Sauce

✳   2 months

INGREDIENTS	Imperial	Metric	American
Cooking apples	*1 lb.*	*450 g.*	*1 lb.*
Water	*2 tbsp.*	*30 ml.*	*2 tbsp.*
Sugar	*2 oz.*	*50 g.*	*¼ cup*
Butter	*1 oz.*	*25 g.*	*2 tbsp.*

Peel and core the apples and cut them into thin slices. Put into a bowl with the other ingredients. Cook in the microwave oven for 3 minutes, stirring twice during cooking. Sieve or blend in a liquidiser until smooth. Reheat in microwave oven for 30 seconds and serve hot with pork or duck.

REHEAT
5 minutes

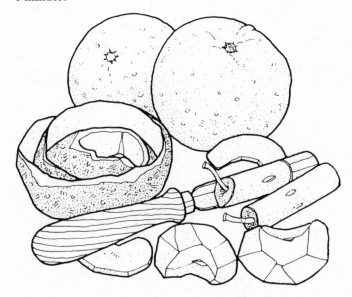

Custard Sauce

INGREDIENTS

	Imperial	Metric	American
Milk	1/2 pt.	300 ml.	1 1/4 cups
Eggs	2	2	2
Caster sugar	1 oz.	25 g.	2 tbsp.
Vanilla essence	Few drops	Few drops	Few drops

Put the milk into a bowl and heat in the microwave oven for 3 minutes. Whisk the eggs, sugar and essence together lightly and pour on the hot milk. Strain into the bowl and put the bowl into a shallow casserole dish containing 1 in./2.5 cm. hand-hot water. Microwave for 4 minutes, stirring 4 times during cooking.

SPECIAL INSTRUCTIONS
Do not freeze.

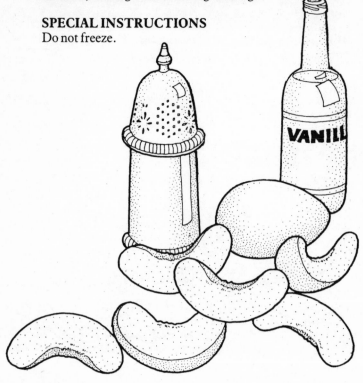

Chocolate Sauce

✳ 2 months

INGREDIENTS	Imperial	Metric	American
Water	1/4 pt.	150 ml.	2/3 cup
Caster sugar	4 oz.	100 g.	1/2 cup
Cocoa powder	2 oz.	50 g.	4 tbsp.

Put the water into a jug and heat in the microwave oven for 3 minutes. Stir in the sugar until dissolved. Microwave for 2 minutes. Whisk in the cocoa powder and microwave for 1 minute. As the sauce cools and thickens, stir occasionally. Serve hot or cold over ices and puddings.

THAW
At room temperature 3 hours
OR
REHEAT
5 minutes

Lemon Butter

✳ 2 months

INGREDIENTS	Imperial	Metric	American
Butter	4 oz.	100 g.	1/2 cup
Lemon juice	1 tbsp.	15 ml.	1 tbsp.
Pepper			

Cut the butter into small pieces and put in a bowl with the lemon juice and pepper. Heat in the microwave for 1½ minutes. Stir well and serve with fish or vegetables.

REHEAT
2 minutes

Butterscotch Sauce

∗ 2 months

INGREDIENTS

	Imperial	Metric	American
Single cream	*1/4 pt.*	*150 ml.*	*2/3 cup*
Dark soft brown sugar	*8 oz.*	*225 g.*	*1 1/3 cups*
Butter	*1 1/2 oz.*	*40 g.*	*3 tbsp.*
Vanilla essence	*Few drops*	*Few drops*	*Few drops*

Stir the cream, sugar and butter together in a bowl. Heat in the microwave oven for 4 minutes, stirring twice during cooking. Stir in vanilla essence. Serve with ices or puddings.

REHEAT
5 minutes

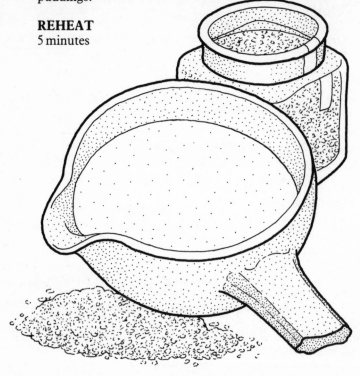

Sweet and Sour Sauce

✳ 2 months

INGREDIENTS	Imperial	Metric	American
Sugar	1½ oz.	40 g.	3 tbsp.
Cornflour	1 tbsp.	1 tbsp.	1 tbsp.
Soy sauce	2 tsp.	2 tsp.	2 tsp.
Vinegar	2 tbsp.	30 ml.	2 tbsp.
Tomato purée	2 tsp.	2 tsp.	2 tsp.
Salt			
Chicken stock	½ pt.	300 ml.	1¼ cups
Canned pineapple, drained	4 oz.	100 g.	4 oz.
Onion	1 small	1 small	1 small
Green pepper	½	½	½

Mix the sugar, cornflour, soy sauce, vinegar, tomato purée, salt and chicken stock and cook in the microwave oven for 4 minutes, stirring twice during cooking. Chop the pineapple, onion and pepper and add to the sauce. Continue cooking for 3 minutes, stirring twice during cooking. Serve with pork, chicken and seafood.

REHEAT
5 minutes, stirring frequently

PUDDINGS

Baked Apples

* 2 months   Serves 4

INGREDIENTS	Imperial	Metric	American
Cooking apples	*4 large*	*4 large*	*4 large*
Maple syrup	*¼ pt.*	*150 ml.*	*⅔ cup*
Butter	*1 oz.*	*25 g.*	*2 tbsp.*

Core the apples without peeling them, and score round the skin with a sharp knife. Put the apples in a shallow dish and pour syrup over them. Put a piece of butter in the centre of each apple. Cover with clingfilm, making two small holes in the film. Cook for 8 minutes in the microwave oven. Serve hot with cream or custard.

Brown Sugar Apples

Prepare the apples in the same way, but substitute 2 oz./50 g./4 tablespoons dark soft brown sugar and 4 tablespoons water for the maple syrup.

REHEAT
5 minutes

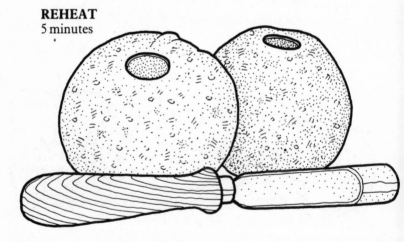

Apple and Apricot Compôte

✳ 2 months   Serves 4

INGREDIENTS	Imperial	Metric	American
Eating apples	2	2	2
Sugar	1½ oz.	40 g.	3 tbsp.
Canned apricot halves	1 lb.	450 g.	1 lb.
Chopped walnuts	2 oz.	50 g.	½ cup
Ground cinnamon	¼ tsp.	¼ tsp.	¼ tsp.
Pinch of ground nutmeg			
Pinch of ground cloves			

Peel and core the apples and cut into thin slices. Put into a casserole dish and sprinkle with sugar. Cover and cook in the microwave oven for 3 minutes. Drain the apricots and stir the fruit into the apples. Add 4 tablespoons syrup from the can. Stir in the nuts and spices. Microwave uncovered for 4 minutes. Serve warm with cream. Canned peach slices, pears or pineapple may be used instead of apricots.

REHEAT
10 minutes

89

Spiced Pears

* 2 months   Serves 4

INGREDIENTS	Imperial	Metric	American
Pears	4	4	4
Red wine	1/2 pt.	300 ml.	1 1/4 cups
Water	1/2 pt.	300 ml.	1 1/4 cups
Sugar	2 oz.	50 g.	4 tbsp.
Cinnamon stick	1 × 2 ins.	1 × 5 cm.	1 × 2 ins.
Cloves	4	4	4
Pinch of ground nutmeg			
Piece of lemon peel			
Lemon juice	1/2 tsp.	1/2 tsp.	1/2 tsp.
Flaked almonds	2 tbsp.	2 tbsp.	2 tbsp.

The pears should be ripe but firm, and even-sized.
Peel them carefully and leave the fruit whole with the
stalks on. Put the wine, water, sugar, spices, lemon peel
and juice into a pie dish and cook in the microwave oven
for 5 minutes. Stand the pears in the liquid with stalks
uppermost. Microwave for 5 minutes. Leave to stand for 5
minutes, spooning the liquid over the pears a few times.
Remove the cinnamon stick, cloves and lemon peel.
Sprinkle each pear with almonds and serve with cream.

REHEAT
10 minutes

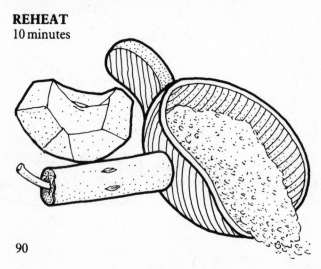

Caramel Oranges

✳ 2 months   Serves 4

INGREDIENTS	Imperial	Metric	American
Oranges	*4*	*4*	*4*
Caster sugar	*6 oz.*	*150 g.*	*¾ cup*
Water	*7 tbsp.*	*100 ml.*	*7 tbsp.*
Orange liqueur	*1 tbsp.*	*15 ml.*	*1 tbsp.*

Peel the oranges carefully, making sure that all the white pith is removed. Cut across in slices and arrange in a serving dish. Sprinkle with the orange liqueur. Put the sugar and water into a basin and stir well. Cook in the microwave oven for 12 minutes until dark golden. Pour over the oranges and chill before serving.

THAW
At room temperature 3 hours

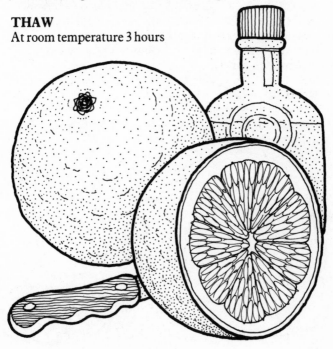

Fruit Sponge

✳ 2 months   Serves 4

INGREDIENTS	Imperial	Metric	American
Eating apples	*1 lb.*	*450 g.*	*1 lb.*
Canned apricots	*8 oz.*	*225 g.*	*8 oz.*
Margarine	*2 oz.*	*50 g.*	*4 tbsp.*
Caster sugar	*2 oz.*	*50 g.*	*4 tbsp.*
Egg	*1*	*1*	*1*
Self-raising flour	*2 oz.*	*50 g.*	*½ cup*
Chopped walnuts	*2 oz.*	*50 g.*	*½ cup*

Peel and core the apples and cut them into thin slices.
Put into a pie dish with the drained apricots and spoon on
3 tablespoons syrup from the can. Cook in the microwave
oven for 5 minutes. Cream the margarine and caster sugar
until light and fluffy. Work in the egg and fold in the flour
and walnuts. Spread over the fruit. Microwave for 6
minutes. Leave to stand for 3 minutes and serve with
cream or ice cream.

REHEAT
10 minutes

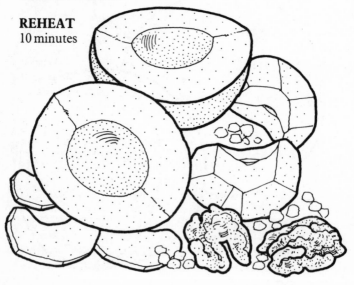

Chocolate Walnut Upside-Down Pudding

✷ 2 months   Serves 8–10

INGREDIENTS	Imperial	Metric	American
Butter or margarine	4 oz.	100 g.	½ cup
Dark soft brown sugar	3 oz.	75 g.	½ cup
Walnut halves	30	30	30
Desiccated coconut	3 oz.	75 g.	¾ cup
Milk	2 tbsp.	30 ml.	2 tbsp.
Plain chocolate	3 oz.	75 g.	3 squares
Self-raising flour	4 oz.	100 g.	1 cup
Granulated sugar	5½ oz.	140 g.	⅔ cup
Baking powder	¼ tsp.	¼ tsp.	¼ tsp.
Bicarbonate of soda	¼ tsp.	¼ tsp.	¼ tsp.
Salt	¼ tsp.	¼ tsp.	¼ tsp.
Vanilla essence	½ tsp.	½ tsp.	½ tsp.
Sour milk	¼ pt.	150 ml.	⅔ cup
Egg	1	1	1

Grease an 8 ins./20 cm. square baking dish and line the base with greaseproof paper. Put half the butter in the dish and heat in the microwave oven for 1 minute. Stir in the brown sugar and spread the mixture evenly over the base of the dish. Arrange walnut halves in this mixture and sprinkle with coconut and milk. Heat the chocolate in a bowl for 1½ minutes until melted. Sift together the dry ingredients and add the remaining butter, vanilla essence and half the sour milk. Beat hard until the mixture is smooth and creamy. Add the melted chocolate, remaining milk and egg and beat until light and soft. Pour into the dish and bake in the microwave oven for 9 minutes. Leave to stand for 5 minutes and turn on to serving dish. Serve with cream.

REHEAT
10 minutes

Rhubarb Crumble

* 2 months Serves 4

INGREDIENTS

	Imperial	Metric	American
Rhubarb	*12 oz.*	*350 g.*	*12 oz.*
Caster sugar	*2 oz.*	*50 g.*	*4 tbsp.*
Water	*2 tbsp.*	*30 ml.*	*2 tbsp.*
Butter	*2 oz.*	*50 g.*	*4 tbsp.*
Plain flour	*4 oz.*	*100 g.*	*1 cup*
Dark soft brown sugar	*2 oz.*	*50 g.*	*4 tbsp.*
Chopped walnuts	*2 oz.*	*50 g.*	*1/2 cup*
Ground mixed spice	*1/2 tsp.*	*1/2 tsp.*	*1/2 tsp.*

Wash the rhubarb and cut into 1 in./2.5 cm. lengths. Put into a pie dish and sprinkle with sugar, and water. Cook in the microwave oven for 5 minutes, stirring twice. Rub the butter into the flour and stir in the sugar, walnuts and spice. Sprinkle on top of the fruit and press very lightly with a fork. Microwave for 4 minutes. Leave to stand for 5 minutes before serving with cream or custard. Apples, plums, gooseberries or blackcurrants may be used instead of rhubarb.

REHEAT
10 minutes

INDEX

Lamb and Potato Casserole 58
Lemon Butter 85

Meatballs in Tomato Sauce 50
Mushroom Stuffed Steaks 57

Orange Glazed Carrots 72

Pitta Pockets 48
Poached Salmon 42
Pork in Cider Sauce 52

Ratatouille 71
Rhubarb Crumble 94
Roast Chicken 69

Sausage and Apple Bake 53
Scrambled Eggs with Prawns 47
Smoked Haddock Pâté 39
Southern Cod 40
Spiced Pears 90
Spicy Prawns 46
Stuffed Baked Potatoes 78
Stuffed Plaice 43
Stuffed Tomatoes 75
Sunday Brunch 61
Sweet and Sour Sauce 87
Sweet and Sour Turkey 67

Tomato Sauce 81
Tomato Soup 35
Trout with Almonds 44
Turkey Bake 65

Veal Stroganoff 59

White Sauce 79